"The forces of darkness figured out a long time ago that they don't have to make any Christian family bad; they just have to make them too busy. It nets out the same effect. It steals the family's joy. Joy is supposed to be the true litmus test of a Christian home. Unfortunately, the hurried lives we live rob families of the one thing that Jesus longed for us to have on a regular basis—rest and the joy that a well-paced family is supposed to gain from it. In *Connecting With Your Kids,* Tim Smith shows you the power of tempo when it comes to deeper and more satisfying relationships. It's a primer for how to slow down, savor the moments, while still getting ahead."

— **Dr. Tim Kimmel,** Author of *Little House on the Freeway* and *Grace-Based Parenting*

"No fewer than eight in ten Americans say they experience stress on a regular basis. This chronic condition of the populace, writes Tim Smith, is taking a serious toll on children and their family life. The author, a youth expert and family coach, has written a book that is must-reading for parents and prospective parents. It offers concrete steps that can be taken to develop the right cadence or pace for family life. His book is a persistent reminder to well-intentioned but sometimes harried and over-committed parents that 'you are what your family wants.'"

— **George Gallup Jr.,** Chairman, George H. Gallup International Institute

"Tim Smith provides parents with a very helpful framework for cultivating closeness and good communication between every member of the family. It's so easy to let the culture set the agenda for family life, and this book helps today's busy parents reclaim control of their time as well as the relationship they've always wanted with their children. I highly recommend this wonderful book!"

— **Wayne Rice,** Director, Understanding Your Teenager

"In a day and age where 'disconnections' seem to increasingly be the mark of families, Tim Smith offers prescriptive help that will facilitate healthy connections and reconnections with your kids."
   —**Walt Mueller,** President, Center for Parent/Youth Understanding

"Time flies—whether or not you're having fun. And it seems to fly faster and faster! *Now* is the time to let Tim Smith encourage and guide you as you slow down and enjoy the adventure of *Connecting With Your Kids.* Don't put it off and let another day fly by!"
   —**Kendra Smiley,** Conference speaker and author of *Aaron's Way—The Journey of a Strong-Willed Child*

"If you are not connecting with your kids, take time to read this light, humorous, simple—yet effective—book. Life is a marathon, and as Tim says, we often try to run it as a sprint in full combat gear! Finally a book that says it is okay to say no to many of the guilt-laden *must do's* and *should do's.* Finding our family's 'heart-print' was an easy and fun activity that we found rewarding and helpful."
   —**Linda Tolosi,** Director of Alumni, Bethany College of Missions

"Reading another Tim Smith book is like having the parent coach right in my living room. With humor, vision, and clarity, Tim takes the seemingly impossible task of *relaxed parenting* and makes it achievable for normal parents like you and me. Tim's lifework has been to remind us of what really matters in our homes; and with *Connecting With Your Kids,* he has done it again."
   —**Mark DeVries,** President, Youth Ministry Architects, and author of *Family-Based Youth Ministry*

CONNECTING _with_ YOUR KIDS

TIMOTHY SMITH

BETHANYHOUSE
Minneapolis, Minnesota

Published by Bethany House Publishers
11400 Hampshire Avenue South
Bloomington, Minnesota 55438

Bethany House Publishers is a division of
Baker Publishing Group, Grand Rapids, Michigan.

Printed in the United States of America

Library of Congress Cataloging-in-Publication Data

Smith, Tim, 1954-
    Connecting with your kids : how fast families can move from chaos to closeness / Timothy
Smith.
        p.   cm.
    Summary: "Connecting With Your Kids challenges life's frantic pace and offers helpful
solutions to slowing down and developing the perfect pulse for individual families"—Provided
by publisher.
    ISBN 0-7642-0131-X (pbk.)
    1. Parenting. 2. Parent and child. 3. Family. I. Title.
    HQ755.8.S6345   2005
    646.7'8—dc22   2005020519

To Denny and Allyson Weinberg

When vision, passion, and need meet,
the impact is astounding.

ABOUT THE AUTHOR

TIMOTHY SMITH is a family coach, conference speaker, president of Life Skills for American Families, and the author of several books, including *Letters to Nicole, Family Traditions,* and *The Seven Cries of Today's Teens.* He is a research fellow with the George H. Gallup International Institute and a radio commentator. He and his wife have two young-adult daughters and live in Southern California.

OTHER RESOURCES BY TIMOTHY SMITH

Parenting tips, books, CDs, and a six-session video series based on the material in this book are available at *www.parentscoach.org.*

Timothy Smith does keynote speaking and presents at family conferences and parenting seminars throughout North America. Find out more by calling toll free 877-376-3500 or by writing Life Skills for American Families at P.O. Box 7736, Thousand Oaks, CA 91360, or check out *www.parentscoach.org.*

CONTENTS

FOREWORD

During the age of the sundial, Sophocles wrote, "Time is a gentle deity." While that may explain how people felt about time during 406 B.C., for those of us living in 2005 and beyond, there is nothing remotely gentle about time. Time stands over a family today and cracks a whip! Everything is moving faster, and almost everyone feels time-strapped. If there's a universal complaint I hear as I talk to families about making changes, it is *"I don't have time!"* There's no time to even think about what we're *not* doing or failing at doing because we've got so much on our plate already! Every single thing on our plate is an "A" item, and we're fighting for every second—and today, seconds count.

For example, did you know that in just three decades, we've seen the average television commercial go from two minutes to fifteen seconds? Who has time today to listen for *two whole minutes* to a sales pitch? And if you don't think you're addicted to speed, think about the last time you got in an elevator. What happens when you punch the button and nothing happens? Ten seconds in an elevator without the door closing is *forever*. Or how long did it take you to go from dial-up to high-speed on your office computer? (Could you even imagine *not* having high-speed at work and, for that matter, at home?)

In the jungles of New Guinea, a missionary friend of ours told my wife and me about a remote village they visited. The entire village was without a single mechanical clock of any kind. Instead, the people there measure their days by "work days" and "rest days." Meaning, you work one day, then you rest the next.

Does that sound like *your* days?

Can you even remember the last time you and your family had a day of rest?

The very thing "fast families" need right now is a book like this that talks our language. That language is *speed.* We need to understand how we've become so hooked on it and, even more important for our family's health, how we can actually slow down enough to hear our family's heartbeat.

Tim Smith has done a wonderful job of giving us extra-busy types a great many on-target insights that don't make a person feel worthless for living a busy life. Nor does he tell us to do something that's simply impossible—like going back to *Little House on the Prairie.* The fact is, there is no going back to an unhurried time.

For example, in 1875 there were over two hundred unique "time zones" across the country. In essence, every major city had its own "standard time." *When clocks don't agree, there's a limit to how fast things can move.* In short, a train might pull in to a station and be on time if judged by the clock in the city where your journey began, and be ahead of time somewhere else, requiring you to wait before pulling out.

As soon as we went on standardized time across our country, the accelerator hit the floor. When you don't have to wait, everything moves toward *now.* And once our entire nation got "on the clock," everything began to be measured first by railroad time, which means "fast," and today, with space travel, supercomputers, and fiber-optic networks, even atomic clocks aren't fast enough to keep up! Now we need "super clocks" that measure time in nanoseconds—measured in *billionths* of a second. What does life speeding up mean for our family?

With all that speed, just to keep up with the new norm, we need two jobs. Night classes to get recertified. Time carved out for church and kids' programs. Choir practices. Soccer leagues.

Helping with homework. In-laws. Bills to pay. Pets to look after. Repairmen to call. We're overwhelmed with so much to do and all of it demanding to be done *right now*.

If that sounds like your family, and if your tongue is hanging out from feeling hurried and harried, then you've picked up the right book. *Connecting With Your Kids* is a must if you want to move from all the rush to genuine closeness, caring, and *rest*.

I've known Tim Smith for years; he has worked and ministered to people who live in the absolute epicenter of what it means to be busy. His insights have helped hundreds of families in the incredibly fast-paced, high-tech world of some of the world's most valued real estate in Southern California. If he can help these cyber-speed families, then whether you live in Manhattan or Missoula, he can help your family as well.

And one last thought in case you're among those who have picked up the book, read this far, and are still trying to decide if you have time to read it. Please don't think to yourself, *Well, that sounds interesting, but I know things will slow down when we or the kids get older.* The fact is, by the time you get to the future (should the Lord tarry), time will have sped up, not slowed down! Here's a sobering thought: The more time that passes, and the more experiences we collect, the faster time seems to pass! Meaning every year you get older, things will speed up for you, not slow down. Just talk to senior citizens today and ask them what it's like having "all that free time," and then watch their eyes roll. If you're looking for a slow-down future to take the time to learn about how to slow down your life to strengthen your family, know that it simply won't come. I strongly encourage you to take the time *today* to start this book—and watch it make a huge, positive, "fast" difference in helping your "fast family" find its heartprint.

John Trent, Ph.D.
President, *StrongFamilies.com*

Start Here

When was the last time . . .

- You saw a child playing catch with his friend, just for fun?
- You saw a child climbing on the wooden play set in her back-yard?
- You saw children laughing, giggling, and sprawled out as they relaxed (without the TV on)?
- You wrestled with your son on the family room floor?
- You played make-believe with your daughter in her room?
- You took a walk with your child for no specific reason?
- You had dinner as a family?
- You felt unhurried, unrushed, and rested?

If it's been a while, then this book is for you.

Don't worry, it won't be about doing more. It will probably be about doing less.

Connecting With Your Kids is about discovering the right pace for *your* family. It's likely to mean slowing the pace, catching your breath, and listening to the rhythm of your pulse.

Can you hear it?

Or are you running so fast—and is the background noise so loud—that you can't hear your heartbeat?

You are not alone.

Families are becoming increasingly busier. In most cases, this adds stress and puts strain on relationships. However, some active families have discovered a rhythmic pace—a heartbeat that works for them.

Connecting With Your Kids is more than a warning to slow down. It's a stethoscope to listen to each family member's pulse and develop a collective cadence that benefits every family member.

A few promises as we go:

- You'll experience a guilt-free zone. I won't be piling on "shoulds" and "coulds." If anything, most parents are already doing too much.
- You'll discover that parenting does not have to take all of your time, energy, money, or emotions.
- We'll challenge the contemporary myth that says, "The natural course of child development isn't enough because, at best, it's mediocre; our kids need a highly programmed dose of 'enrichment.'"
- You'll see that your common sense and natural parenting instincts are the best tools you have—trust them. You don't have to fear your kids. In fact, tentativeness deprives them of needed confidence and security.
- You'll find out why we rush.
- You'll encounter applicable principles and practical ideas that will help you ease up on the intensity of a frantic pace and be delivered from the parent's perennial to-do list.
- You'll discover a cadence that is right for you and your family.

Connecting With Your Kids is divided into four parts:

Part One deals with *Breathless Pounding*—a look at restless families and why most of us seem to be on the run.

Part Two, *Check Your Pulse,* helps us take a look at the heart of the matter—how to connect with your child, heart to heart.

Part Three will help you *Discover Your Heartprint*—your

unique pace as well as your child's. We'll define and examine four different heartprints.

Part Four brings it all together with *Making Your Heartprint Work for Your Family,* presenting tips and recommendations for connecting with the various heartprints.

Are you ready? Pour yourself another glass of iced tea, and then let's discover why so many families are hurried and what we can do about it.

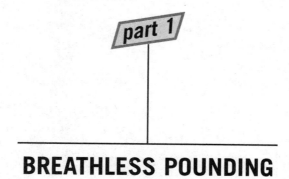

BREATHLESS POUNDING

CHAPTER ONE

Restless Families

You might be a fast family if . . .

- You've tried to enter your password on your microwave.
- You have fifteen phone numbers to reach a family of three.
- You call your son's cell to leave a voice mail—"It's time to eat"—and he text-messages you back from his bedroom, "What's for dinner?"
- "Cleaning up the dining room" means getting fast-food bags out of the SUV.
- Your daughter is selling Girl Scout cookies through her Web site.
- "Family dinner" is saying grace after ordering at the drive-through but before paying at the first window.

Again, you aren't alone—most of us are feeling hurried. While living at a fast pace isn't necessarily bad, being negatively stressed is. More and more families are reporting that they feel restless.[1] I have liberating news: Good parenting doesn't have to be exhausting. In fact, good parenting may actually involve doing *less*!

CARMEN'S DISCOVERY

When I was presenting my seminar *The Relaxed Parent* to a lively group near Tampa, one of the moms introduced herself during the break.

"I wanted the best for my son and my daughter. I wanted to

give them everything, especially the things I didn't have as a child." Carmen brushed her perfectly coiffed black hair behind her ear, revealing a brilliant diamond-stud earring. "When they were in preschool, I learned about all these *enrichment* opportunities. The other mothers couldn't believe I didn't have the kids signed up, so I quickly got them enrolled in dance, art, karate, soccer, and gymnastics. The pressure was immense. I don't know why, but we all believed that if some enrichment activities were good for our kids, then *more* enrichment activities would be even better."

"I know what you mean," I said, nodding in agreement, sipping my soda. "It's so easy to get snagged by the 'good parents are always busy' trap. What happened next?"

"With one child it wasn't too bad, but with Alexis's demanding schedule added to Jacob's, it got to be too hectic. Something had to give, and it was going to be my marriage. *Thankfully,* I was able to talk with my husband about the issues, and we worked through them. You know, I don't think our kids appreciated being that 'enriched.' We decided they only needed one activity at a time, so we narrowed it down to karate for Jacob and dance for Alexis. Now we have a sane schedule and a stronger marriage."

"So what do you do with your extra time?"

"Twice a week I organize a pickup soccer game for the neighborhood kids at our park. Girls and boys play together. No need for uniforms, seventy-five-dollar fees, referees, or practice. All we need is a ball!"

"Super idea. Would you share it with the other parents after the break?"

"I'd be glad to. I've enjoyed your seminar so far. It's encouraging to discover that you can be relaxed *and* be a parent. I'm delighted to learn how to carve out time for my children to be children."

"You are courageous, Carmen. Many parents feel the pressure from other parents and are unwilling to face the criticism they might receive, like, 'You're pulling Jimmy out of hockey?! Are you trying to handicap him? You've got to give him every possible chance to succeed!' I'm glad you've learned *and* applied the truth that pulling back doesn't necessarily mean we're losing anything; it just means we're seeking to be strategic."

After Carmen shared her story, I continued that theme with the whole group. Busyness does not make a more capable child. A child does not always need more activity or more enrichment, but he does need one thing—more of you! *You are what your child wants.* Not karate, vocal training, football, or cheerleading.

Try smiling at your daughter when she enters the room. Do your eyes light up when you pick up your son from school? Our children need our time and attention more than they need structured activities. Solid family bonds are the most important factor in a child's life.

You—yes, *you!*—may be the most enriching aspect of your child's life. Don't sell yourself short. A generation ago the latchkey kid was the poster child for neglect; nowadays it might be the overscheduled child who never rests but is shuttled from activity to activity.

Sometimes doing more for our children may mean doing less.

HECTIC HOMES

If you have kids, you're probably tired. I know, that's an exercise in "observations of the obvious," but research does back me up on this one. A Gallup poll[2] in 2002 revealed that in families with young children, stress from being hurried is as common as ground-up Cheerios in the carpet.

About 40 percent of Americans indicate they have limited

amount of time to relax, including 14 percent who say they *never* do, and only 30 percent feel they have adequate relaxation time. Of all working mothers, 65 percent report that they "never have" or "have little" time to relax; working fathers aren't too far behind, with 55 percent giving the same response. More than 60 percent of single parents with young children and single-income marrieds with young kids also report that they don't have enough relaxation time.

Working moms clearly are the most stressed—only 9 percent say they have sufficient time. Children require a lot of our time and energy. Young children, in particular, diminish or even eliminate spare time.

Many of today's well-intentioned parents act like chauffeurs, shuttling their school-aged kids to piano, Scouts, soccer, then church activities . . . even on the same day. Family life often revolves around scheduled events, rather than the events fitting around the family's schedule. We used to be able to count on Sundays as days of rest, with no practices, games, or other non-family events on the calendar. Now Sunday is seen as just another day, jam-packed with all forms of activity, religious and secular.

Today's homes are hectic in part because our children's involvements compete with each other. One mom told me with a wry smile, "It's a good thing I'm not divorced; I couldn't get these kids to all of their games on a weekend. It takes Bob and I all of Saturday and Sunday just to cover the bases, and even then I sometimes have to ask a friend to help."

Have you noticed that each coach or trainer or instructor thinks that her endeavor is the most important and that it must be given top priority? Wouldn't it be refreshing to hear from one of them, "Hey, come to practice whenever you can—after all, its just baseball, and Sammy is only seven. He'll have plenty of time to work on his skills. All we're trying to do now is make it fun."

Facing a growing number of mutually exclusive requirements, family traditions like dinners, barbeques, weekend trips, and vacations are the first things to be sacrificed for the pursuit of excellence in our competitive culture.

The result?

Frenzied and under-connected families.

The irony is that I've met dozens of parents who undeniably feel overwhelmed but still don't sense that they're doing enough for their kids. In the next few chapters we'll explore why we cram our lives with so many elective commitments, but now I want to make sure to emphasize the effects that a hurried lifestyle has on both children and parents.

HURRIED HEARTS

First we learned that cholesterol, found in many of the foods we eat, is bad for us. Then we were told, "No, it isn't." Then reports said that some cholesterol is good and that some is bad. I still don't know too much about cholesterol, but I do know that the things I like most—bacon, donuts, fried chicken, and mashed potatoes swimming in gravy—have never been on most physicians' recommended list. Though this isn't a diet or health book (we *will* discuss food and our hearts), it seems plain that overeating fatty foods tends to clog up our arteries and slow down our heart's effectiveness.

The heart is basically a pump. Excess cholesterol in the body is deposited as plaque on the walls on the arteries, restricting the pump's outflow. Our overly busy lives are somewhat like this plaque—the busyness may be as tasty as pastries, but ingesting unreasonable amounts of it can be unhealthy and damaging.

Hurriedness has a negative impact on at least three areas of life. *Rushed living clogs up our lives and robs us of enjoyment, effectiveness, and energy.*

Enjoyment

Allen settled back on my office couch with his wife, Elaine, next to him. He cleared his throat and continued: "I'm so upset with him, but I don't know what to do about it. Seems like he only thinks about himself."

"Oh, that's not true, Allen," Elaine said. "He'd love to spend more time with you. He's just being a typical twelve-year-old." She looked to me for confirmation.

"Cody does sound fairly normal," I concurred. "He seems to look for ways to get time with you. He mentioned paintball, motorcycles, and body-boarding as activities he'd like you to do together."

"Yeah, I know." Allen looked down at his shoes. "But I work such long hours. I leave at six and I don't get home until after eight, and I'm just wiped out. Relating to Cody is so much energy—everything he wants to do is some extreme sport! The kid has every toy imaginable—snowboard, body board, two motorcycles, scooter, mountain bike, go-kart, basketball hoop, swimming pool, video games, computer. I don't understand why he isn't satisfied. I didn't have any of that stuff when I was his age."

"Does he have friends?"

"Yes, he has lots from school and sports," affirmed Elaine. "One close friend, Jimmy, lives right down the street."

"Speaking of Jimmy," Allen said, "on Saturday, I was trying to do some work on my home computer and Cody kept interrupting me. Finally, I told him to go to Jimmy's and he said he was too tired to walk and asked for a ride. I thought he should get the exercise, so I told him no. I still can't figure out why he didn't just take one of his five motorized toys."

All I could think at this point was, *five motorized toys!* Why does a twelve-year-old need five? (Allen had only mentioned four, at any rate.) "Perhaps Cody wanted you to drive him to Jimmy's because he wanted to be with you?" I said.

A puzzled look spread across Allen's face. "Do you think so?"

"He was buggin' you to spend time with him on a Saturday. That's why he was reluctant to go to Jimmy's. He probably sees Jimmy all week; on weekends, I'm guessin' he'd like to be with you."

"That's what I've been telling you," Elaine added.

"I know you work long hours to provide for your family, Allen, but sometimes they don't need more stuff—they need *you.*"

He picked at a tiny spot on his chinos. "We have a garage full of toys that we bought to do together—I even have my own motorcycle—but it seems like all that stuff doesn't bring me and Cody together. I never have time to use it. We haven't gone riding since last year; he goes with Jimmy and his dad."

"Is your busyness robbing you of enjoying life, for yourself and with your son?"

"Yeah, it is."

Allen offers a compelling illustration of how hurried lives miss out on enjoyment. His long, demanding workdays (plus a one-hour daily commute) weren't entirely needed, and his accusation of Cody only thinking about himself was accurate: Cody learned it from Allen. Allen wasn't happy with the accoutrements of success: fashionable clothes, luxury car, fancy outings, high-end vacations, expensive hobbies. None of these were bringing him enjoyment.

You know you're too busy when the very things you're working so hard to attain fail to bring you enjoyment after you acquire them.

Effectiveness

Watching the most recent Super Bowl reminded me of our national obsession with winning. To get the Vince Lombardi trophy, a team needs to win enough regular-season games to make the playoffs . . . then win its conference . . . then win the Big One . . . and *then* they can be called winners.

But are all of the other thirty-one teams really losers?

I think we need to redefine our definition of success. We need to reconsider our fixation on ultimate victory and what it truly takes to earn the label of "winner." Perhaps, like Allen, many of us also need to acknowledge that success at work doesn't mean success at home.

Are enormous aspirations actually best for us and our families? Are they worth the cost? Consider these thoughts from Alvin Rosenfeld and Nicole Wise:

> We sure do love our winners here in America. We clap hard for our sports heroes, our business moguls, and our entertainment celebrities. In our own lives, we push hard and place a high premium on success. It may be, though, that our sky-high hopes and dreams pitch the path to happiness too perilously steep; many of us cannot climb it without great anxiety and distress. While some people unquestionably thrive on the challenge of working hard to get to the top, a larger percentage likely would find that, in the end, a less pressured life is more meaningful and gratifying. It is true that great cultural rewards come with reaching the summit. But striving for it full time—and that's

often what it takes—may throw our lives way out of balance.[3]

Success may have more to do with effectively balancing demands and priorities than simply winning. I believe that a single mom who balances the demands of working, caring for her children, maintaining a household, and still taking time to relax on weekends by taking her family to the park is a *huge* success. In fact, she's a model for all of us: she's learned to manage, rather than just compete, at life.

Energy

Frantic lives rob us of precious energy. Some of us felt overwhelmed at the very start—just the thought of becoming a parent was draining!

But now that you *are* a parent, are you pacing yourself for the long haul? Parenting isn't a one-hundred-meter dash but a marathon, complete with hills and valleys and unexpected detours.

Some of us are breathlessly sprinting, with sweat dripping into our eyes and blurring our vision. *Where is the finish line? I didn't realize the race was going to be this long. I don't think I'm going to make it!*

Our current frenetic parenting is a product of our age, engineered in a high-tech environment with exacting standards. Our fears and desires are exploited by savvy marketers who peddle the latest *must-have* trends. The parenting popes publish *must-do's* via Web sites, magazines, and books. The pop psych gurus admonish us with the latest *must-be* hype from their TV and radio studios. Nearly everything in our culture is designed to communicate three simple words to parents: "A little more."

A little more information.

A little more time.

A little more enrichment.

A little more "age-appropriate" education.

A little more stimulating experience.

A little more kindergarten readiness.

A little more college readiness.

A little more adds up to a *whole lot.*

And it's driving us nuts!

Let's keep going to find out why.

DISCUSSION QUESTIONS

Parent to Parent

If possible, connect with another parent for a few minutes to discuss the following:

(1) Describe a funny incident that occurred when you were too hurried (maybe something like those listed at the beginning of the chapter).

(2) What are some ways to escape the "good parents are always busy" trap?

(3) Discuss this statement: "*You* are what your child wants."

(4) In what ways have you experienced "success at work doesn't mean success at home"?

(5) What are some "a little more's" that influence us? What can we do to reduce or cut off the enticement and impact of the ones our families don't need?

Parent and Child

(1) Share the personal aspects of Carmen's discovery (above) and ask, "What could we do to play together like she and her family do?"

(2) Talk about the differences between being relaxed and being lazy.

(3) Ask what your child imagines you doing with your time all day.

CHAPTER TWO

Why Do We Rush?

"I can't remember the last time I felt rested," said Amy, a forty-something mom. "I like your couch. Mind if I stretch out and take a nap?" Her smile morphed into a yawn.

"Be my guest—might be the most refreshing forty-five minutes you have all week."

She raised her eyebrows. "Actually, I'm here to see you for coaching. I want to get organized, personally and with my kids."

"What are some of your challenges?" I asked.

"Well, just keeping up with three children—two in grade school and one in middle school. Even though I work full time, I can usually adjust my schedule to attend their games and after-school activities. But I think my restlessness is catching up with me. I feel irritable, I can't concentrate, I'm not as productive at work, and my husband thinks I've been snippy with the kids."

"How much sleep do you get?"

"Five or six hours a night."

"This isn't rare, Amy. Moms seem to be the sleepiest of all Americans. Did you know that the National Sleep Foundation says women are twice as likely as men to complain about not getting enough sleep? In fact, three out of four women get less than the recommended eight hours per night."

"But I'm not growing—at least *up*. Why do I need eight hours? I thought that was just for kids."

"Well, even most teens aren't getting enough sleep; some try to function on six hours when they actually need nine or ten. Sleep is important for women, because at every stage you face complex physical and biological changes, any one of which can ruin a good night's sleep. Pregnancy. Babies. Menstruation. Toddlers. Menopause. Teenagers. On top of all of that, more women than ever are dealing with the pressure of intense jobs, relational barriers, financial stressors, and single parenthood. It all adds up to a huge energy drain."

"Tell me about it." Amy fluffed the pillow and reclined deeper into the couch.

"We used to brag about our busyness and our disregard for sleep, like those were noble badges of honor. Now we realize their unhealthiness. Adequate sleep all by itself enhances relaxation, efficiency, and effectiveness. Being rested allows you to find enjoyment in life; by contrast, even small issues seem large when we're constantly fatigued."

"I've noticed that the tiniest things are bugging me. I mean, I'm stressing over the carb count in my kid's sack lunch."

"And he probably doesn't keep all of it anyway—probably even trades up for Ding Dongs!"

"See, I'm obsessing over stuff that doesn't matter. What can I do?"

"Amy, you're at the stage of motherhood where day-to-day demands are usually the reasons for loss of sleep, but sometimes it's more than that. Let's start with the obvious. Working moms usually don't get enough sleep because they're overcommitted."

She nodded in agreement and offered a wry smile.

I went on. "For instance, many moms develop an active alert response to any sounds their children make at night. The resultant hypersensitivity causes them to wake easily and not experience the deep, restorative sleep they need."

"I do get up in the middle of the night and check on them. Most of the time it's nothing."

"So you start out the day tired?"

"Exactly. But how can I change it?"

"You probably need to make sleep as important as other needs in your life. You will have to cut out something else in order to recapture the time."

"It seems like everybody wants me to go faster. Everywhere I turn I hear, *Speed it up! Do more! You can make room for one more thing!* I've had it. Why do we always rush?"

I liked Amy's provocative question. Why *do* we always rush? Dr. Phil McGraw helps to clarify the challenge before us:

> Cynics will tell you that in our fast-paced society "family" is becoming obsolete, that it is just an old-fashioned, lost concept, getting buried in a busy world of "enlightened" people. I'm here to tell you that that is not right, not even close. Family is even more important today than in generations past, and its erosion is unacceptable.
>
> This is a fight we can and must win. This is a fight we will win if we just do our homework and plug in. As a parent you have the power to set your child on a course for success. You may or may not feel powerful right now, but if you have the courage to rise to the challenge, your child can and will be blessed beyond belief. . . .
>
> It is our duty as the leaders of our families to make sure we are counteracting rather than contributing to the craziness.[1]

Family is *not* obsolete. Family is still the best way to raise kids, develop civil citizens, enjoy marital permanence and stability, and pass on a legacy. In spite of social scientists and others deriding family, nobody has come up with a better idea.

Yet our own schedules could be the primary enemy. Most of us are simply too busy. Studies show that since 1960, children have lost ten to twelve weekly hours of time with their parents.[2]

Why *are* we so busy?

I believe there are at least seven reasons why we're in such a rush. We'll deal with six in this chapter and then devote chapter 3 to the seventh.

Our Culture Cherishes a Fast Tempo

We live in a culture fascinated by speed. It's the *latest* fashion, the *late-breaking* news. Can you imagine watching a commercial that barks, "It's last year's styles, stale as can be, coming to a thrift store in your neighborhood!" Or "We'll have film at eleven of footage we found in the archives of Walter Mondale's Greatest Speeches!"

Who cares, right?

We live in a culture obsessed with *new*. Who's dating whom? What's the most recent DVD release? Who's hot, who's not? What's #1 on pop's Top Forty? For hobbies like sports, we can be updated virtually anywhere, 24/7—during pretty much every one of each day's 86,400 seconds—on almost any result, standing, injury, or transaction. We want everything immediately, and we want everything immediately accessible.

Commerce Compensates Quickness

It wasn't long ago that if we "absolutely, positively need it overnight" we'd ship a package via FedEx. We still do, but that's slow compared to e-mail, fax, instant messaging, text messaging, or video conferencing. Our standards for excellence and for pace have gone up concurrently in proportion. We expect most things to be done flawlessly and finished within the hour (quicker if possible).

Business transactions occur so rapidly that we now expect to get far more accomplished in a day. For many of us, the workday seems to be creeping more and more into our personal time—starting earlier, ending later, and still around when the weekend arrives.

Most companies reward speed with promotions, accolades, cash, stock options, and incentives. Can you imagine a boss announcing, "Congratulations, and a bonus, to Bill—he told me the Sheffield account can wait because he's going home at five to see his daughter's soccer game. What a team player and thoughtful father!"

Bill more likely will get furrowed brows and critical comments from both colleagues and supervisors. In many business cultures, family, at best, is tolerated, viewed as a necessary evil that deters efficient commerce.

Media and Technology Promote Speed

Have you ever bought a brand-new computer with all the options, only to have it become outdated within a matter of months? Frustrating, isn't it. Technology is developing with such absurd speed that even engineers and designers who work in the field are hard-pressed to keep up.

Emerging innovations have an impact on us. We feel we need to maintain the pace—the pace of business, the pace of relationships, the pace of communication, the pace of information exchange in general. We don't want to be hamstrung by being stuck with outdated equipment. We could still hack out memos and speeches on manual typewriters and have them slowly delivered via first-class post. Some still do. But why, we wonder.

Technological advancement creates a false gallop that we feel compelled to match, even if we sense in advance that our gait will exhaust us long before we finish the race. Various forms of media not only support the pace but also promote it. With satellite this and wireless that, our electronic secretaries give us the less-than-delightful opportunity to be digitally pestered at any moment of any day (or night), anywhere in the world! You can be backpacking in the Rockies and get live-action feeds of terrorist activity in the Middle East on your handheld PDA. The globe is truly our theater.

Our Families Fuel It

Keeping up with the Joneses has become a full-time job. We don't want to be the last family on the cul-de-sac without the must-haves. Because media is so pervasive and marketing so effective, each family member is bombarded with myriad, nearly omnipresent messages of "You really need this because (insert one or more of the countless reasons here)."

"Don't wait to ask your doctor about Zoopidor," the pretty lady in the field of tulips advises me in a neighborly tone. Now I feel like I might need Zoopidor, and I don't even know what it's for. I was feeling fine until that pitch. Suddenly I wonder, *Is there something wrong with me? If there is, could Zoopidor help fix it? I'd better ask my doctor just to be safe—what if I don't check into Zoopidor but then I find out I need it?*

The ads are carefully crafted to create a need. Once marketers establish a perceived vacuum in our lives, they will be able to fill it with their products. That's why, after hours of TV, we usually feel at least somewhat more restless and discontented. Commercials are designed to provoke us, worry us, and make us think we need something we maybe didn't even know existed.

Television families generate discontent as well. Even when they have challenges and conflict, they're able to resolve everything in twenty-two minutes or less, wrapping it all up with a touching final scene containing the requisite laughter and hugs.

This tends to leave us thinking, *What's wrong with my family? We're never like that.*

Media exploits the family; then the family fuels culture's hectic velocity.

Our Selfishness Demands It

I hate to say it, but sometimes it comes down to old-fashioned selfishness: "I want it all; I need to experience it all; I don't want to miss out."

We overbook our lives because we want to. We want it for ourselves, so we squeeze it in, charging it on the credit card or by some other creative means.

Why?

Because we want to and we choose to.

Greed nourishes speed. Because we want something and want it now, we become gripped with the desire for immediate gratification.

Several years ago I was introduced to some of the reasons we rush in Tim Kimmel's classic *Little House on the Freeway.* Kimmel presents one particular reason so well:

> The truth is that I don't need society, a job, or even the media to create a hurried home. I can do a great job of it on my own. Man's fleshly ego *hungers* for an overloaded life. We become addicted to regular surges of adrenaline.
>
> Our hurried lifestyle is a result of taking shortcuts in life. *Since the fall of man in the Garden of Eden, sin has refused to let us rest.* (emphasis added)[3]

Stripped to its core, sin is the demand to have it now. Sin is the enemy of time. Organization takes time. Meaningful communication takes time. The development of intimate friendships takes time. Building character in a child takes time. Conversely, warped by sin, our egos look for cheap shortcuts, and by circumventing time, we end up profoundly restless and dissatisfied.

Our hurried lifestyle is nothing new. Ever since Adam and Eve blew it in the Garden, we've been in a rush to get to the next thing, the next level, the next fruit (forbidden or not). Our sinful nature torments us with an obsessive drive toward activity and experience rather than contentment and rest.

Debt Drives It

One of the primary reasons Americans work increasingly longer hours is the attempt to deal with our consumer debt. Because of the five preceding reasons for why we rush, many of us overextend our credit or tax our family budget just to make room for a new car or for new wood floors.

I often coach dads and moms who both work at least sixty-hour weeks, try to be involved with their kids, get things done around the house, and "make it better" for their children than what they had while growing up.

Harvard University psychiatrist Robert Coles calls this the "teddy bear syndrome."[4]

> Some of the frenzied need of children to have possessions isn't only a function of the ads they see on TV. It's a function of their hunger for what they aren't getting—their parents' time. Children are no longer being cared for by their parents the way they once were. Parents are too busy spending their most precious capital—their time and their energy—struggling to keep up with MasterCard payments. They're depleted. They work long hours to barely keep up, and when they get home at the end of the day they're tired. And their kids are left with a Nintendo or a pair of Nikes or some other piece of crap. Big deal.

The majority of Americans believe that economic pressures

mean more family members need to work harder. Listen to what sixteen-year-old Ken told me during a recent coaching appointment:

> I have to work. My dad is out of a job for the third time in five years; my mom works full time but only makes nine dollars an hour. If I want to buy anything I have to use my own money. I have to save up for my own car. My dad drops me off at work and my mom picks me up after I get off at ten. I'm so tired from working twenty-five hours or more a week. I usually fall asleep in first period. My parents are mad about my grades, but I don't have time to do homework.

Ken is from a typical middle-class family in a comfortable L.A. suburb.

The pressure to keep up has taken time away from the family, which in turn has caused a decline in the quality of family life, a weakening of family values, a descent in satisfaction with one's own family, and an increase in life's constantly accelerated pace—*just to keep up.*

An Antidote to the Rush

Two nights a week Karri and Robert dim the chandelier, put on soothing light jazz, and sit down to eat by candlelight, using their china and crystal.

It's not a romantic dinner.

Not even close, because their two children join them. Five-year-old Andrea and nine-year-old Bobby help set the table.

Karri and Robert have two jobs, two kids, two pets, and too little time. Until a few months ago, their evening meal was survival of the fittest—everyone reaching for what they wanted and gobbling it down before heading out. Then I met them and suggested the concept of family dinner.

"Now we enjoy real conversation and we actually relax. By making time for each other, there's less squabbling. The kids are better too," said Karri.

"It seems to help us unwind and tune in to each other. I've actually felt more relaxed, and I even sleep better on those nights," added Robert.

"I'm glad you're doing this," I affirmed. "Study after study finds that kids who eat dinner with their families regularly are better students, healthier people, and less likely to smoke, drink, or use drugs than those who don't."

Robert winced at the thought of his kindergartner being associated with those vices. "If all it takes is saying no, turning off the TV, and letting the answering machine pick up, then I'm all for it. Who would have thought something as simple as family supper could mean so much?"

A University of Michigan study of children aged three through twelve found that more meal time with the family was the *single strongest predictor* of better achievement scores and fewer behavioral problems—even better than time spent studying or in church.[5] So dust off the nice dishes, dig out the candles, crank up the Crockpot, and gather round the table!

DISCUSSION QUESTIONS

Parent to Parent

1. Describe the last time you felt truly rested. How did it come about, and what made the difference?
2. Why do you think we're tempted to present our hectic pace and lack of rest as noble badges of honor?
3. Why is the family still viable and not obsolete?
4. Of the six stated reasons why we rush, which do you most

strongly identify with, and why?

5. What might be effective for you in challenging these six reasons for rushing?

Parent and Child

1. At your children's ages, how much sleep should they get? Why? How can you know if they're not getting enough sleep? Discuss with them.

2. If your children are old enough, introduce them to the above six reasons for why we rush. Ask, "Which of these have you seen in your life? In our family?"

3. Discuss the idea of a family dinner, complete with candles, music, nice dishes, etc. Ask your child, "Would you like this?" "How often?" "What should the rules be?" "How can you help?"

CHAPTER THREE

On the Run

We rush because others are rushing.

We rush because we are rewarded when we do.

We rush because in our culture, speed has a higher value than patience.

We rush because it makes us feel important.

We rush because we want to run *with* others and run *to* something.

In the previous chapter we examined six reasons why we rush; now let's look at perhaps the biggest:

We rush because we are running from *something.*

Following my presentation to a large group in Minneapolis, as the emcee wrapped up the meeting, I walked toward the back of the room to stand by my resource table. An attractive thirty-something woman with short dark hair quickly approached, her forehead wrinkled and her cheeks dripping with tears.

"Thank you for your . . ." she sniffed, dabbing the corner of an eye and then her salmon-colored nostrils with a tissue before continuing. "I really needed to hear what you said today. I've decided that I will be the last 'crazy' in my family. I'm not going to pass on the lunacy I grew up with to my kids."

As she paused, I noticed her carefully tailored gray suit, designer shoes, and matching handbag. I reached for her hand. "I'm Tim, thanks for your kind words."

"I'm Anna," she said as she offered a firm shake. "Sorry

about . . ." She pointed to her face and made a circle. A large diamond and sapphire ring adorned her finger. "I've been driven to succeed ever since high school. I got good grades, went to university, and now have a successful business. I'm the envy of my siblings and old friends, but I'm not happy. In fact, I'm afraid to be alone or be still.

"I'm haunted by my own thoughts and feelings: *I'm not smart enough. Not pretty enough. Not rich enough. Not creative enough.* But I know the reason I work so hard is that I'm running from the pain of my family. Dad divorced Mom when I was twelve. He left when I needed him the most. He never saw me dress in a gown and go to the prom. He never told me I was beautiful. His distance sent me on this mad obsession to capture his attention. I felt like I had to have money and power to earn his approval. Thanks for helping me see that my frantic efforts are really just diversions."

Anna is not alone in her frenetic pursuit. Many of us are terrified of stillness, of quiet places. We're afraid that if we stop, painful memories or uncomfortable feelings will encroach. And so we keep busy—very busy. Too busy for us to feel or to remember.

LIFE IN THE FAST LANE

In my family-coaching practice I've met many pleasant, successful people who don't know how to rest—they're always on the go. This lifestyle has its acknowledged rewards. They *are* often rewarded with promotions and payoffs for their dedication (some schedule sixteen-hour days into their PDAs).

Even so, the downsides to obsessive activity are remarkably high for these go-getters. They pay the cost of jam-packed weeks and weekends. They commonly have trouble with relationships because of their task orientation. Many have lost their marriages.

Some have difficulty maintaining friends. Their intensive project-at-hand focus sidelines others who aren't part of their current venture. They feel guilty when they relax or, as they call it, "do nothing."

But the saddest consequence for fast-lane drivers—by far—is the detrimental impact their crazed pace has on their children. They model at least three wrong beliefs:

1. "You are what you do, so get busy."
2. "Rest and relaxation aren't that important."
3. "Relationships exist for what you can get out of them."

Children aren't as ignorant and unobservant as we think (or hope). They know these messages are false.

Their response? They might react by dragging their feet and procrastinating. After all, *not* doing as you're told gets you attention, even if it's not warm and fuzzy. They may also sense that grades are important to their parents, so they study inadequately (or not at all) to retaliate or to create drama. Others, of course, do far worse to send the message, *"Notice me!"*

When kids observe their parents relating to their adult friends, they often note (for example) the difference between a genuine friendship and a contractual, networking relationship. If all they ever see is their parent (or parents) "working" others for gain or benefit, not only will they thereby learn the fine arts of manipulation and posturing, but *they will also try the very same approach on their parents.* Most often, teens eventually stop challenging these misleading behaviors in and false messages from their parents; they learn that they're not being heard, so instead of resisting they start to adopt the same approaches. Surprised and angry parents frequently contact me, the family coach.

One over-busy mom complained, "I can't believe how self-centered and heartless our son is! All he wants to do is be with his friends. He's always going somewhere. He never has time for us. If we let him, he'd be out every night of the week."

A fast-track dad fumed, "Our fourteen-year-old has done some incredibly vicious things to her 'friends,' and they do it right back. I had no idea girls could be so cruel to each other. All they do is use each other. But in spite of all that pain, she still has to be with her group. She doesn't want to do anything with us, including our family vacation!"

Many parents have similar gripes. Are some of them reaping what they've sown?

SENSELESS STRESS

My issue isn't with the pace of life—it's commendable to be efficient and productive in short order. My concern is with *purposeless pounding*. Running itself isn't problematic; the problem is running on a treadmill—that stressful hammering of the feet against a conveyor belt taking us nowhere.

This is exactly how many of us are living life, as individuals and within our families. The *family* is stymied, generating lots of activity but not moving forward. We are sweating and breathing hard while not ever leaving the gym. We're missing the joy of the journey because *we've replaced adventure with activity*.

The treadmill (or the more en vogue elliptical cross-trainer, which stimulates a sort of cross-country skiing) may well be the icon of this millennium's initial years. Craziness isn't necessarily advancing us. We know we're supposed to exercise thirty minutes a day, several days a week, but that's hard to fit into our crammed schedules; when we shift a half dozen items on the itinerary and get down to the health club, we discover others just like us—frantically bouncing up and down or sprinting like greyhounds chasing the elusive rabbit. These days we even need diversions while exercising: my club has two hundred different channels on over a dozen TVs!

What would happen if we got off the family treadmill? What might take place if we aimed for an actual destination instead of purposelessly jogging in place? Maybe we'd look (and *be*) more like travelers and less like hamsters.

My goal is to help you get off the treadmill—running, not getting anywhere—and place you on the track, heading toward meaning and purpose.

First question: Which would you say best represents your life in the last three months—treadmill or track?

RUNNING TO WIN

My high school and college cross-country teams would warm up before a race by jogging the course backward. We wanted to spot the hills, drops, and curves from a different perspective; we didn't want to get lost or inadvertently cut the course and be disqualified. Our three- to six-mile races presented a variety of loops, turns, and other potential hazards; fatigue made it easy to make a mistake and somehow get sidetracked. After attacking the hills, jockeying for position, and racing till our lungs screamed, getting even slightly off course would be a huge waste—all of us feared running well for miles but then missing the last turn. We ran to win, strategically, with purpose and discipline.

Many of the activities of running families are noble and well-intentioned, yet their movement is aimless. They're treadmill runners, and they aren't in the race. They won't make it to the finish line because they aren't on course. Consider Paul's words in 1 Corinthians 9:24–27:

> Remember that in a race everyone runs, but only one person gets the prize. You also must run in such a way that you will win. All athletes practice strict self-control. They do

it to win a prize that will fade away, but we do it for an eternal prize. So I run straight to the goal with purpose in every step. I am not like a boxer who misses his punches. I discipline my body like an athlete, training it to do what it should. Otherwise, I fear that after preaching to others I myself might be disqualified. (NLT)

You can't tell who will win a long-distance race by examining the starting line: Everyone looks like a runner. No matter the lightweight tops, running shorts, running shoes, and black chronograph watches—*what determines true distance champions is how they finish.*

Why is it that some don't finish well or finish at all?

Running to win means running with purpose and with self-control. Families that win have these very qualities. They aren't sidetracked by diversions or detours. They don't get pulled off course through errors caused by weariness because they face their issues and thus don't haul around extra weight in the form of unnecessary baggage.

We live in a multiple-option culture. Even the most minute of endeavors seems to entail the possibility of myriad choices, and the sheer magnitude of the menu can be overwhelming. We can develop headaches just trying to select our entertainment! Nevertheless, having so many options doesn't mean we have to select any of them. Many of us are longing to slow down, even a little.

THE SIMPLE LIFE

Presenting my parenting seminar in rural Indiana, I noticed a couple entering forty-five minutes late. She wore a head covering and a pale cotton dress that went to midcalf. He wore black boots, a muted, lightweight flannel work shirt, and dark pants; a mustacheless beard on his chin underscored his engaging smile.

As they vigorously took notes, she nodded with agreement when I spoke about the influence of media and culture on today's kids.

Afterward I introduced myself.

He smiled and shook my hand. "We apologize for being late. We got here as soon as we could."

"Thank you for your presentation," she added. "We learned much. We want to do well with our children. Our oldest is fifteen, and we're concerned." Her creamy face was youthful, without a wrinkle or any sign of makeup.

"I'm glad you made the effort to be here, and pleased to know it was helpful."

"We'd like to buy these," she said, producing a stack of my books. "Would you please autograph them?"

"Gladly." I signed them and handed them back.

"Again," said the man, "please forgive us for being late. We came from Kokomo and I drove the buggy. Blessings." He shook my hand as they left.

The host of the seminar, observing this exchange, came over and said, "They live at least fifteen miles away. It must take them an hour to get here by buggy."

I thought about this fine Amish family. Their life is, by design, *simple*. No technology. No phone, TV, radio, or Internet. No distracting material temptations seducing them to validate their membership in our consumer culture. Yet even out of clan-centered, uncomplicated living, they were eager to learn how to positively counteract societal influence on their children and discover more about how to be effective parents.

I took home a lesson from the heartland: We need to ruthlessly challenge *anything* that seeks to make our family life more burdened. We need to passionately value simplicity. We need to valiantly fight complexity.

You don't line up to run a 10K with combat boots, a backpack, and a weight belt. But many families essentially do this with their lives. They try to run with unnecessary baggage.

We need to run light if we are to run with endurance.

> Since we are surrounded by such a huge crowd of witnesses to the life of faith, let us strip off every weight that slows us down, especially the sin that so easily hinders our progress. And let us run with endurance the race that God has set before us. We do this by keeping our eyes on Jesus, on whom our faith depends from start to finish. (Hebrews 12:1–2 NLT)

Most weights we carry seem ultimately to serve *some* good purpose, but ultimately they will slow our progress. Hebrews encourages Christians to "strip off *every* weight that slows us down." Note that these don't have to be sins—they can actually be laudable activities, relationships, hobbies, or possessions—but if they're distractions from what matters, they need to be unloaded. Sin, missing the mark of right living as defined by God, can be anything that slows us down, gets us off course, or distracts us from "keeping our eyes on Jesus" . . . the goal . . . the finish line.

As a long-distance runner, sometimes the only way I could find motivation to persist and endure the pain was to imagine reaching the finish line. The Christian family needs to keep its eyes on Jesus the entire race—from start to finish. Doing so enables us to learn to detect the weight slowing us down and the hurdles of sin lurking in front of us. Even when we're unaware of these barriers, they exist, and each of us faces them; running with focus teaches us to concentrate and to discern.

MOM CHARGERS

I often refer to over-busy parents as "chargers." Many *mom chargers* had mothers who told them, "Idle hands are the devil's workshop." Buying into the ethic that busyness is next to godliness, they often believe that *if activity is good for me, then more activity is better.*

As a result, many moms tend to be over-producers, squeezing as much activity as possible into every day, shoehorning their schedules, multitasking, and then multitasking the multitask!

Over-producers tend to see life like a checkbook: "If I still have checks, I can write them." Most don't see life like a bank statement: "How can I make more deposits and fewer withdrawals on my time and energy?"

I know of one hectic mom who schedules her day in fifteen-minute blocks, beginning at 5 A.M. and ending at midnight. Her PDA (personal digital assistant) barely has time to recharge before she resumes her rigorous routine the next morning.

Our friendly automakers have created ubiquitous vehicles for mom chargers: minivans and SUVs have actually become mini-motor homes, complete with TVs, DVD players, stereos, refrigerators, and storage for snacks and several changes of clothes. Mom also has an arsenal of office gear so she can multitask with her cell phone, files, tablets, PDA, laptop, and GPS to talk with those clients . . . *and* find those out-of-town soccer fields.

A 2002 CNN/*USA Today*/Gallup poll reports:

> Parents of young children, especially working mothers, are most likely to say they have little time to relax. A person's work status is also strongly related to stress, as those who are employed full time are among the most stressed group of people. Retirees and older Americans, not surprisingly, have the least amount of time pressure in their daily lives.[1]

What's the key to stress relief? What's a parent to do?

For starters, take time to evaluate: *Why am I so rushed?* It may be due to one or more of the reasons we've examined. It could also be that you are seeking to escape. Through my research and in my family-coaching practice, I've discovered that moms tend to avoid three tender topics.

Running From the Past

The first area a mom may seek to avoid is *pain from her family of origin*. She may have hurtful experiences from her childhood; neglect or wounds; criticism (past or current) from her mother or father. Any of these issues (and other leftovers) can compel a mom to keep busy enough not to address them, for avoidance seems easier than dealing with long-term pain or disappointment.

I like the TV show *Everybody Loves Raymond*, but sometimes Ray's mother, Marie, really annoys me! She's tough on Ray's wife, Debra—no matter what Debra does, she can never satisfy her mother-in-law. Living under a critical eye is excruciatingly difficult. In almost every episode, Debra expresses the frustration of seeking to please an unpleasant parent.

Many women are faced with similar situations. They have family members who gossip or speak harshly or act apathetically. Sometimes it's easier to stay active than to risk criticism or rejection.

Before you dismiss this as a possible reason for rushing in your life, consider these thoughts from marriage expert Harville Hendrix:

> When you hear the words "psychological and emotional damage of childhood," you may immediately think about serious childhood traumas such as sexual or physical abuse or the suffering that comes from having parents who divorced or died or were alcoholics. And for many people this is the tragic reality of childhood. However, even if you were fortunate enough to grow up in a safe, nurturing environment, you still bear invisible scars from childhood, because from the

very moment you were born you were a complex, dependent creature with a never-ending cycle of needs. And no parents, no matter how devoted, are able to respond perfectly to all of these changing needs. . . .

Even though our parents often had our best interests at heart, the overall message handed down to us was a chilling one. There were certain thoughts and feelings we could not have, certain natural behaviors that we had to extinguish, and certain talents and aptitudes we had to deny. In thousands of ways, both subtly and overtly, our parents gave us the message that they approved of *only a part of us*. In essence, we were told that we could not be whole and exist in this culture.[2]

You may be an over-producer mom seeking approval from your mother or father. Looking for them to notice. Desperate to hear them say you are pretty enough . . . smart enough . . . capable enough . . . or *I'm proud of you*. You haven't yet heard it in a way that satisfies and soothes your soul; because the silence is deafening, you fill it with the cacophony of endless pursuits.

Running From Disillusionment

The second reason a mother may keep too busy stems from being *disappointed with her husband*. At the core of each of us is the desire to return to the Garden of Eden, where man and woman, husband and wife, live in abiding intimacy, reveling in a peaceful oasis, unencumbered with clamor. Today's wife and mother realizes this is not her life, and it bothers her.

Many of us enter marriage with the expectation that our spouse will magically recapture this emotion of devotion, this cosmic connectedness, this unique understanding. Then reality comes crashing in: he tracks dirt all over the house; she doesn't record checks in the register; he burps in front of dinner guests;

she snores so loudly that she wakes the kids—the *neighbor* kids.

And intimacy goes out the door.

No one wants to connect with an ill-mannered, inconsiderate baboon. But having the expectation that my spouse will take me to Eden is unrealistic, a common reason for marital unhappiness and discontent.

If you're disappointed with the level of closeness you're experiencing with your husband, don't run away by building a life apart from him, consumed by children, work, or hobbies. Pull out the wedding album and reflect on those early days when you had time to take walks and eat dinner unhurriedly whenever you wanted. Ask him, "What can we do to recapture those moments now? How can our hearts and minds be joined even in light of our other responsibilities?"

It takes time to slow down and connect. It also takes courage.

Running From the Kids

A third reason for insane motherly busyness is that *she doesn't know how to have a genuine connection with her children . . . or she doesn't want one.* I know, it seems harsh, but hear me out.

Some moms get outdoors in Nikes and Lycra, pushing high-tech strollers. It's actually a creative way to multitask: She gets exercise, the kid gets fresh air and time with Mommy. But what about the moms who talk on their cell phones during the entire outing? Or listen to the radio with headphones? Or go only if they can be accompanied by a friend with her own Humvee-sized stroller (complete with cup holders for lattes)? Are they really enjoying the bonding of a shared mother/child experience?

Some moms are actually afraid of being alone and being quiet with their children. However, this is one of the best environments to bond with babies and to fondly reconnect with children. Those silent, unrushed, uninterrupted moments when Mom has time to stroke her child's hair and cuddle with him on the couch are nourishing for both.

NORA'S DILEMMA

"It's easier for me to be at work than at home with Darrin," Nora admitted. "I trained for years to be an attorney, but I have no preparation to be a mom. It doesn't come naturally to me. It's easier to keep busy than to slow down and 'bond.'

"I'm embarrassed to admit it," she confessed as she raised her eyebrows and frowned. She brushed imaginary lint off of her tailored and trendy navy business suit. "I only wanted one child and we had him late. It's probably a good thing."

Her eyes drifted to the window. "I don't know if I have what it takes for one, let alone two or three. Some days I come home from work too exhausted to listen to a third-grader's ramblings. Too distracted to understand what he wants. I don't always have the energy to care. . . . Am I a bad mom?" She reached for a tissue and dabbed at the corner of her eye.

"No, you're not a bad mom. You're here, aren't you? You're trying to learn. You want to grow to be better as a parent."

"Yeah, I do."

"I'm glad. Tragically, sometimes we unconsciously pass on our own childhood wounds to our kids. It tends to be a lunacy or a legacy."

She smiled. "With my family, it's definitely a lunacy."

"But you don't have to pass on that same craziness to Darrin. The first step is to take time to evaluate why you parent the way you do. We frequently overcompensate for what we didn't get from our parents; we're determined to make it happen for our kids. In some cases, we unknowingly imitate our parents and re-create the same painful situations. The key is to stop and ask, *What needs to get carried on and what needs to stop?*"

"I do both," she said with a nod, exhaling heavily. "I grew up with very little; they called us 'trailer trash.' My father was always losing his job. I was determined to do better for my son. That's what drives me to work long hours—long *billable* hours." She grinned. "But I also realize that in the midst of my frantic pace, I can't meet his emotional needs. I've given him stuff, but I haven't given him *me*."

"Sounds like you *are* imitating your parents."

"Yes. They were consumed with making ends meet, and I'm consumed with fifty billable hours a week; either way, you're consumed."

"Nora, I've observed two kinds of imbalance in this regard. The *fuser* mom is too attached to her child and lives her life through him; she's afraid of any independence. The *isolator* mom unconsciously drives others away, even those she loves, and keeps them at a distance; this gives her a sense of control and helps her achieve tasks but ultimately makes her lonely."

"That would be me."

HOPE FOR MOM CHARGERS

Perhaps you identify with Nora; maybe you distance yourself from those you love, even your children. Or you might be too close to the kids—you'd even follow them around all day if allowed. In either case, there is hope for you. As we unpack the principles for dealing with our hectic homes, take a few minutes by yourself. Fix your favorite drink, prop your feet up, and ask yourself, *Why do I parent the way I do? What do I want to pass on from my parents? What do I not want to pass on from my parents?*

Imagine a simpler life. What would it look like for you? Chances are, you could use some fine-tuning (without having to become Amish).

DAD CHARGERS

It's culturally acceptable for fathers to be busy—they are to be the providers first and the nurturers second. This norm has created a haven for dads to hide out, often cramming their lives with activities because they're racing *from* something. "I have too much work, dear. I won't be able to spend time with the family this Saturday." *Men have learned that they can get away with using rapid pace to avoid connection.*

Our society tends to teach boys tasks and girls relationships. As a result, our young men are growing up without the skills they need to navigate relational challenges. When they become adults, the cultural myth is reinforced with *you are what you do,* and many young men become consumed with their jobs. Ambition and industry are commendable, but using work to evade relationships, particularly those in a family, is risky and hazardous.

Dad chargers also use technology to sidestep intimacy. Most guys don't need much of an excuse to be fascinated with the latest high-tech device; we generally love to vanish indefinitely into cyberspace and the tantalizing world of the emerging *latest.* I like to go into stores that sell cutting-edge products and watch men become immersed in the bright lights, the beeping tones, and the captivating smell of fresh plastic and bubble wrap.

I must acknowledge a personal weakness. After I recently finished a game-room addition on our house, all I needed was the monster TV with high definition. My buddy Dan and I ventured down to the electronics superstore that promised to have "your big screen in time for the big game." I was excited to hear about their no-payments-until-the-next-geologic-era plan; I was enthralled with the new technology.

Right before me were the brightest, clearest, loudest, and hugest! The store was dimly lit, except for the pay-through-the-nose-here counter, which was under intense halogen wattage that generated enough heat to slow-cook pork ribs on the Formica.

I stood frozen, awestruck by the pulsating screens. *Which of these behemoths will fit? How do I know what to buy?* Too many capital letters were thrust in my face: HDTV; CADTV; CRT; WEGA; OPRAH; LSMFT. The audio/video guru quickly sensed my angst and offered to guide me through the maze of machinery and toward a "state-of-the-art solution for my family's viewing preferences and needs."

I left with pink and yellow duplicates totaling a half ream of paper and a promise that my grand eye-popper 2007XL would be shipped and installed before the big game. Meanwhile, I was welcomed to return and visit the floor model so we could bond.

(I did.)

Other useful diversions for too-busy dads are tools and toys. I particularly enjoy browsing the power tool section of my local home improvement warehouse, a pile of noise-generating machines with lots of horsepower. I don't know the purpose of many of these impressive steel weapons, but that doesn't keep me from admiring them. Remember those hilarious episodes of *Home Improvement?* Tim "the Tool Man" Taylor's invariable tweaking of some implement to have "more power" resulted in magnificent disaster. That show's popularity came from striking a powerful chord with American men—it featured power tools!

Tools are to many men what shopping is to many women. We don't have to buy mechanical gadgets to enjoy entertaining their possibilities. We love holding them, feeling their weight, testing their grip, and imaginatively inventing projects that would actually require the seven-hundred-dollar device in our sweaty palms.

Tools can serve as a handy diversion. They aren't flaky and unpredictable like humans. If we buy the quality brands, we can expect durability, reliability, and high performance. If only we could expect the same from our closest relationships! When men decide that they can't, they hide out with their tools and fill up their schedules with projects: *anything* to avoid conflict.

Men love their toys too; toys provide recreation *and* create distance. When women are sitting and talking, the average man is likely driving (or wishing he were driving) a vehicle as fast as possible, preferably not on a road.

One husband who thoroughly enjoyed jet-skiing with his wife exclaimed, "We scream across the water at forty miles per hour, and we don't even have to talk! She's on her watercraft and I'm on mine. It was perfect. Then we had kids. Now she wants to sell the jet skis and get a pontoon boat—so the kids can come along, and so we can talk."

HOPE FOR DAD CHARGERS

NASCAR is enjoying a surge in popularity throughout the country, and fans of racing know that even a champion driver takes pit stops. If you're a charging dad, speeding through your days like you're in a stock car, consider downshifting your high-performance, turbo-charged self and swinging into the pits. Take ninety seconds to swig some Gatorade and wipe the sweat off your brow. Let your crew slap on some fresh rubber and tweak the spoiler. Take a deep breath and listen to a few questions through your headset:

"Why does racing feel so good?"

"Why do I feel better going fast?"

"How do I use technology, tools, or toys to divert myself or keep busy?"

I know your intentions are good—you work long and hard because you want to provide for your wife and kids. But could you benefit by receiving some input from your Manufacturer?

You'll never know the performance you can get until you follow the Designer's specs.

DISCUSSION QUESTIONS

Parent to Parent

1. In what ways are you like Anna, filling your life with frantic efforts that are really diversions?
2. What are some life-in-the-fast-lane rewards? What are some liabilities?
3. How do you know if you're on a treadmill instead of on a track?
4. Discuss this quote: "*Running to win* means running with purpose and self-control. Families that win have these very qualities."
5. Have you longed for the simple life? Describe any of your thoughts, feelings, observations, and convictions.

Parent and Child

1. Retell the story of the tortoise and the hare. Ask, "Why is it important to remember that *slow and steady* wins the race?"
2. Practice "running with weights." Give your child something relatively heavy (but unbreakable) and ask him to carry it through a short running course (e.g., around the yard). Then give him something very light (e.g., a feather). Then discuss Hebrews 12:1 and ask, "What are some weights that slow us down in life?"
3. Discuss one of these three wrong messages we convey to our children: "You are what you do, so get busy"; "Rest and relaxation aren't that important"; "Relationships exist for what you can get out of them." Why are they inaccurate?

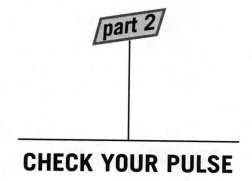

part 2

CHECK YOUR PULSE

CHAPTER FOUR

The Heart of the Matter

I was trying to schedule a time to meet with Barbara's sixteen-year-old son. She called me on her cell phone, desperate for help: Brandon was irritable, mean to his little sister, and argumentative with both parents, she reported. "I hear you're a family coach and can help us. How soon can we get him in?"

"When is he free?"

"Well, let's see . . . he has guitar lessons at one, water polo at three, and youth group at seven; on Thursdays he doesn't have group but he has a tutor come at six; do you have 8 P.M. open a week from Thursday . . . oops, can you hang on? I'm getting another call."

Making an appointment with someone in today's average family can be more challenging than scheduling the Summer Olympics!

Stress has become a common part of North American family life. The demands of work, home, family, and everything else place an increasing burden on everyone, including children.

The same CNN/*USA Today*/Gallup poll reported that more than six out of ten Americans indicate they have a limited amount of time to relax, including 14 percent who say they never do.

- o 41% say "I frequently feel stress daily"
- o 37% say "I sometimes feel stress daily"
- o 78% (combined) feel stress on a regular basis[1]

The question asked on the survey was:

Think for a moment about how busy your schedule is throughout the day, both at work and outside of work. On a scale of 1 to 5, where 1 means you never have any time to relax, and 5 means you have as much time as you need, where would you place yourself?

- 14% recorded 1—"Never have time"
- 26% recorded 2—"Rarely have time"
- 30% recorded 3—"Sometimes have time"
- 11% recorded 4—"Usually have time"
- 13% recorded 5—"As much time as needed"

Only *9 percent* of working moms say they have enough time to relax. Among working dads, only 55 percent report that they have even a limited amount of relaxation time. A majority of mothers not working outside the home say they have limited relaxation time. In fact, the seven groups with the least amount of time to relax all have young children.

From all this research, we conclude: *Kids stress us out and sap all of our time!*

Brandon and I finally got together. On his second appointment, he shuffled into my coaching office, staring at the floor and keeping his hoodie on in spite of the ninety-degree heat. When he sat on the couch he looked out the window.

"Hey, Brandon. Wanna soda or water?"

"Water would be cool."

I grabbed us a couple bottles from the fridge and returned; he was still staring through the window.

"Thanks." He began to guzzle.

"It's hot out there. They say you should drink lots of water, keep yourself hydrated."

"Yeah, our coach is always on us about it, especially if we're sittin' out in the sun at a tournament."

"How long have you been playing water polo?"

"Since I was eleven. Started in a club. Been playin' ever since." He shifted in the couch and took off his shades. Thin dark circles ringed his blue eyes. The weariness of a middle-aged man peered back at me, dull and drained.

"How are things going since we talked?"

"Not much better."

"Glad I could be of so much help." I raised my eyebrows, smiled, and sipped my water.

"I didn't mean it that way. I meant . . . well . . . at least now I understand why things are the way they are."

"It's cool, I was just messing with you."

"There's just too much stuff going on. Sometimes I just wanna chill, but my mom has an agenda for me. It's always something. I wish she'd give it a rest."

GIVE IT A REST

We all know what stress feels like: headaches, sleeplessness, neck and back tension, shortness of breath, stomach pains, heart palpitations. Brandon's stress was manifesting itself through irritability and aggressiveness. His mom, without being aware of it, was contributing to the problem. Overscheduled kids are actually more at risk than their less frenetic counterparts.

Dr. Alvin Rosenfeld, child and adolescent psychiatrist, coauthor of *The Over-Scheduled Child—Avoiding the Hyper-Parenting Trap,* and, perhaps most important, a father of three, says, "This isn't just a matter of over-the-top parents. This is a serious national issue. We are doing, with the best intentions, real damage to our kids and to our families."[2]

Recent medical and psychological studies report that over-scheduling can damage our health and our marriages and compel our children into depression and risky behaviors involving drugs, alcohol, and sex. Other related indicators of stress include compulsive behavior, sleep disturbance, a drop in grades, withdrawal, tantrums, hostility, and acts of violence. Some kids have been scheduled so much that they don't know how to entertain themselves and play or relax on their own.

We want the best for our kids, but in the name of enrichment's pursuit we can actually delete important elements of their lives. Over the past twenty years, free playtime for kids has dropped by 50 percent, while time for structured activities has soared. Family dinners have decreased by 33 percent. When they were kids, baby boomers had 250 percent more free time for play than kids today. Today, the additional time with our kids is likely to be driving them from activity to activity.[3]

One summer, Suzanne and I were delighted to go on vacation to the British Virgin Isles. After an intense time of speaking, followed by meetings at a publishing convention in Atlanta, we flew into Tortola. As soon as we got off the plane we were greeted with the Caribbean's striking beauty, heat, humidity, and slowness!

The first thing we did was stand in line for thirty minutes at customs—primitive, slow, inefficient, low-tech, and *perfect*! I needed a buffer to slow up and wind down. I needed to hit the pause button.

The transport to the resort took longer than I anticipated, so I savored the splendor of the crystal clear water as we drove only a few feet from it. Checking into the hotel also took longer than what we expect in the U.S., as the friendly personnel simply worked at a languid pace. They took time to chat with guests, greet fellow workers, and enjoy the exquisite surroundings.

At first I felt bothered, but I began to realize I could learn something. *Embrace the pace that's given you* seemed to be their motto. My anxiety hadn't normally succeeded in speeding things up anyway—whether on a Caribbean island or in L.A. freeway traffic—so I might as well go with the flow.

With undeniable difficulty, I didn't look at my PDA for a week. We didn't have a schedule, itinerary, or list of tasks. My primary concern was to pad on down to the beach breakfast buffet before it closed at ten-thirty.

It was the perfect getaway for Type A's like me!

On a sailing and snorkeling day-trip, we learned from our guide that *tortola* means "tortoise." Aptly named, for the islanders have discovered that hurrying around doesn't always make a difference—and that when it does make a difference, the difference isn't often positive. Plus, when you're on an island you can't go too far anyway!

Regardless, I believe we place too much value on the speed of convenience. We like fast food, fast mortgages, and fast computers. We pay dearly for everything that promises to be a timesaver, while such items frequently cost us more time than they conserve.

My time in the Isles taught me the value of *slow*. I experimented with walking more slowly . . . talking more slowly . . . eating more slowly . . . generally, *searching for the true value of waiting*.

Remember "Slow and steady wins the race"? Our island neighbors are on to something, living in contrast to the mainlander lifestyle that teaches us to take pride, to find virtue, to mark importance, to obtain merit in *being busy*.

Want to do something unique? Next time someone asks you, "How are you doing?" try saying, "Great, not too busy." It may feel weird, since it's probably not a familiar experience, but if you learn to do it repeatedly, saying *and* applying it, you can learn to live in a way that affirms we don't always have to be busy.

HAVE A HEART

In the Bible, *heart* is mentioned 667 times! Scripture isn't referring to the organ that pumps blood through our bodies; "heart" is most often an expression for our deepest, innermost thoughts and feelings.[4] Today, when we say a person has *heart,* we are generally indicating his wholehearted commitment to a challenge or endeavor. Such devotion engages the whole person— mind (intellect), will (volition), emotion (feeling), and conscience (moral sense).

> Love the LORD your God with all your heart and with all your soul and with all of your strength. (Deuteronomy 6:5)

Why is the heart important?

Because it influences the thoughts we entertain, the choices we make, and the feelings we acknowledge and embrace. The heart impacts everything.

> Above all else, guard your heart, for it is the wellspring of life. (Proverbs 4:23)

> Keep vigilant watch over your heart; *that's* where life starts. (Proverbs 4:23 THE MESSAGE, emphasis added)

Scripture also cautions parents: don't break your child's heart. You *will* disappoint her; you *will* have to say no, and at times he *will* hate you for it. That's part of being a parent. But I'm not speaking of crossing a child's will; I'm talking about *breaking the will,* about causing him or her to *lose heart.*

> Parents, don't come down too hard on your children or you'll crush their spirits. (Colossians 3:21 THE MESSAGE)

We crush the spirits of children when we're too hard on them, expecting perfect behavior, perfect grades, or perfect performance.

We crush their spirits when we're too easy on them, ignoring bad behavior, giving in to whining, or failing to instill civility.

Remember playing on swing sets or jungle gyms at school? Did you ever fall and have the wind knocked out of you?

I did.

What do you need when your wind gets knocked out?

Multiple choice:
A. A lecture on swing-set safety
B. A scolding for not wearing shoes with better grip
C. A training video on how to recover your wind
D. AIR!

When you get the wind kicked out of you, the only thing you need, the only thing that helps, is getting the wind back in you. Yet so many parents emotionally knock the wind out of their kids, causing them to lose heart.

> Don't exasperate your children by coming down hard on them. Take them by the hand and lead them in the way of the Master. (Ephesians 6:4 THE MESSAGE)

This book is about parenting in a way that *leads* our children and doesn't *exasperate* them. The prefix of the word *exasperate,* ex, comes from its Latin root, meaning "to take out of." The suffix comes from a term we've heard on *ER:* "We need to aspirate this patient, stat!" Meaning, "give him air." Exasperating our kids is knocking the wind out of them, keeping them from what they truly need.

The Top Ten Ways to Frustrate Your Kids
1. Don't bond with your young child by giving him physical affection, time, and attention.
2. Believe that professional child-care providers are an adequate substitute for your relationship with your child.
3. Don't cuddle, read, talk with, or play with young children.
4. Ignore all the fuss and hassle about rules, routines, and discipline.
5. Don't bring your moral and spiritual values to your child. Let her discover them on her own.
6. Give your child plenty of freedom and control over his own life.
7. Live your life through your child. His success is yours; his failure is yours. His performance should help you feel secure.
8. Never allow your child to be held accountable by having to experience consequences for her behavior.
9. Expect the best even in areas where she isn't particularly gifted.
10. Don't waste your time talking about issues of importance.

ENCOURAGING YOUR CHILD'S HEART

Don't forget: being a child can be scary. A child constantly encounters situations never before experienced. Everything is new. Our kids need *encouragement,* which is *the art of pouring courage into a child's heart.*

Kids can gain courage when they're around us. They become more secure if they know they're important enough for us to invest time with them. But this does take time.

Before you sign up your child for synchronized swimming or Dog Sledding 101, take a few minutes to evaluate the environmental impact on your family. We encourage our kids when we consider the weight that activities entail in their lives and ours. We discourage them when we're inconsiderate.

The *Family Consumer Guide to Kids' Activities,* published by Putting Family First, a movement dedicated to helping parents balance family time with outside activities, offers a few questions to consider before enrolling children in an activity:[5]

Before You Sign Up, Ask:
1. How does the activity affect all family members?
2. Will it interfere with meals, bedtimes, vacations, religious observations, holidays, and family commitments?
3. Is it about winning or having fun?
4. What are the benefits of participating now and in the future?
5. Are there apt to be unanticipated costs or time commitments?
6. How much time in the car will it require?
7. What are my obligations as a parent?

8. How can I support the adult leader's efforts?
9. Whom can I call with my questions?

LET'S HEAR IT FOR FREE PLAY!

In contrast to *organized play*—team sports, artistic lessons, and other enrichment activities—unorganized, unstructured *free play* is essential. Make sure your child isn't so overscheduled as to not have time for play.

Stuart Brown, psychiatrist and founder of the Institute for Play in Carmel Valley, California, warns,

> It is not wise to neglect play. Play has a profound influence on the social, emotional, and cognitive development of kids, but our society has tended to trivialize play and not recognize its significance from early development on. Only now, through an increase of scientific study, are we starting to ferret out play's underlying, and critical, importance. *Free play instills lessons and life skills* that span myriad fronts: self-esteem; empathy for and the ability to cooperate with others; the ability to create, innovate, and work outside the proverbial box. Free time is also dream time.[6]

I agree, and I have a question for you, dear parent: Wouldn't it be awesome to work at the Institute for Play?

"Going golfing?" your wife asks as you head out with your clubs.

"No, doing *research* at the Carmel Valley Country Club, then on to the Institute to continue my project on which game is more fun—basketball, volleyball, or team handball."

"Don't work too hard."

Now *that's* a job!

Free play needs to be part of your child's day. Play isn't optional. *The child's economy is play.* A child trades in play. A child's capital is time to play.

The parent's economy is financial, but children don't think this way. They judge what's important by how it impacts their play: "We had a fun time at Ian's because he has a new basketball hoop and we can lower it and I can dunk! It's soooo cool! I wanna go back. We played for three hours."

Notice he doesn't mention anything about the cost.

LET'S HEAR IT FOR BOREDOM!

Yeah, I can hear you groaning from here! "But what about my kid whining that he's bored?"

Boredom isn't all bad. Right now, in our society, boredom is experiencing a challenging time with public relations. Repeat after me: "Boredom is my friend."

Again, "Boredom is my friend."

Good!

The beauty of boredom is that it constrains kids to think, to imagine, to be creative. It inspires them to be innovative and resourceful. Don't feel guilty when your child plays the boredom card—you might just be helping her to experience the environment in which she learns how to paint, or write a story, or design another world (made in the backyard, out of cardboard boxes, with the intention of escaping her mean parent!). Don't give in to the temptation to labor overtime to earn money for the toy he *had to have* . . . then discards after five days. Encourage him to use and develop the inestimable resources he has inside.

Science backs me on this one. A poll conducted for the Center for a New American Dream reported that 90 percent of children aged nine to fourteen say family and friends are "way more important" than things money can buy. Six out of ten kids say they'd rather spend time having fun with their parents than shopping at the mall. One in four said the lack of family time is because their parents are too busy with work; one in five blamed their own busy schedules.[7]

Instead of staying all evening at the office to provide stuff and pay for activities, get those boxes, go out in the backyard, and play with the kids!

Hang-Time: Ideas for No-Agenda, Free Playtime

If you're stuck and can't figure out what to do, consider some of these suggestions. (More also available in the appendix.)

1. Develop an *Anti-Boredom Rx.* With your children, make a list of at least ten things they can do when they get bored. When appropriate, join them with the prescription. Example: Make a miniature tree house for dolls, modeled after *Swiss Family Robinson.*

2. Invite a few friends from school to join your family in a game of *Sardines.* Secretly appoint one person to be "it." Turn out all the lights in the house; "it" hides somewhere. One by one, everyone else finds her and hides with her, smashed together like sardines. The last person to find the group gets to pick the next "it."

3. *Porta-Party.* Fill a cardboard box with candy, soda, decorations, noisemakers, and any party stuff you have around the house or can get at the dollar store. Throw in your favorite table game, pick an unsuspecting family of friends with children about the same age as yours (probably works best with later grade schoolers and middle schoolers, i.e., ages ten to fourteen), and surprise them with a visit. Say, "We brought our *Porta-Party* and want to have fun with you! Got ice?"

DISCUSSION QUESTIONS

Parent to Parent

1. What are some ways that busyness and overscheduling have kept you from creativity and imagination in your family life?
2. What frequently or sometimes keeps you from enjoying time with your family?
3. Discuss this statement: "Some kids have been scheduled so much that they don't know how to entertain themselves and play on their own."
4. What do you think about the above list of *The Top Ten Ways to Frustrate Your Kids*?
5. If a child's economy is play, what are some ways you can increase the likelihood of free play and reduce the demands and costs of scheduled, organized activity?

Parent and Child

1. If your child is old enough to understand the concept, ask, "How do you like to relax? When do you feel the most relaxed and not pressured?" You may be surprised by what you discover. If possible, try to make sure her preferred style of relaxation happens this week.
2. Designate thirty minutes as "Mommy Time" or "Daddy Time." This is when you get to sit in the hammock or recliner and relax. Nothing is expected of you! Ask your child(ren), "What will you be doing for thirty minutes that won't disturb me?" Set a kitchen timer and instruct: "Please don't bother me or make any demands or loud noises while I'm having Mommy Time. You need to stay at this table and quietly color until you hear the timer go off." By setting this boundary, you're modeling a healthy lifestyle and teaching your children both to control their demands on you and to rest themselves.

3. Before you enroll your child in an organized activity, review with him or her the above suggestions from *Before You Sign Up, Ask.*
   - "Does this activity make scheduling problems for your brother or sister or mom and dad?"
   - "Does it get in the way of our family meals, your bedtime, or other important things?"
   - "Is it about winning or having fun?"
   - "What will you do to make things easier on the whole family if we sign you up for this activity?"

CHAPTER FIVE

Turning Your Hearts Toward Each Other

"Hey mon, you need to pace yahself, to get into the rhythm," said Felix, a fifteen-year-old from the Caribbean island of Roatan. We were cutting back the jungle from creeping in and swallowing the school where he was a student, and I was his teacher.

In my early twenties, I thought speed and power were the way to attack the forest with a machete; the locals had a rhythmic cadence that allowed them to work for hours. We'd been chopping for less than sixty minutes and I was dripping with sweat. I stopped, straightened out my aching back, and watched the islanders sweep their blades across the heavy grasses, vines, and roots.

It looked like a martial arts ballet. With a gentle sweep to the left, they'd switch the direction of the tool, then sweep with their backswing to the right. Slowly, methodically, and in unison they cut; *I* was out of sync and out of breath. They frequently stopped, chatting as they ran a sharpening stone against their machetes. After a few minutes, they returned to their work.

That day I learned a huge lesson for life. Frequent resting restores energy and permits time for honing. Productivity is enhanced not by rapid power or by continuous work but by consistent pace marked by periodic breaks. By taking the breaks and talking about fishing, soccer, or even who had the biggest muscles, my young islander friends also recharged their engines—their bodies.

We often restore our strength in the company of our friends. Hopefully, we renew our energy in the company of our family. *Rest is essential for connecting.* We can't always *build* relationships; sometimes we have to *grow* them. It's slower and not as observable, but it is foundational to having family relationships that outlast the creeping vines of our cultural jungle.

Rest, pace, and connection are praised in the sacred Hebrew writings:

> GOD, my shepherd!
> I don't need a thing.
> You have bedded me down in lush meadows,
> you find me quiet pools to drink from.
> True to your word,
> you let me catch my breath
> and send me in the right direction.
> (Psalm 23:1–3 THE MESSAGE)

The Good Shepherd leads us to rest. (Notice David does not say, "You give me strength to run in place.") Thankfully, He leads me to quiet rest—moments free from striving and lack. In that "moment" He *restores my soul*—renewing my body and spirit by reordering me with divine serenity.

> Come to me, all of you who are weary and carry heavy burdens, and I will give you rest. (Matthew 11:28 NLT)

Our families are in *desperate* need of renewal and rest. One of the most accurate symbols for today's common family is a runner out of breath.

We need to catch our breath and be turned in the right direction.

A CADENCE FOR CONNECTING

Growing relationships cannot be done at broadband speed. What's the best pace for connecting with our kids? It will be different for each child and family, but generally the best pace is slower than what you usually offer. Our kids are simply not as enamored with our to-do lists. They aren't as wrapped up with tasks. They're more concerned with relationships, and those take time, can be messy, and don't always follow a schedule. They're watching us to see what we do. Alvin Rosenfeld says,

> When you rush around delivering them to a conga line of activities . . . it tells them we want them to be hyperactive, overachieving, over-scheduled workaholics, and that's what they could very well become as adults.[1]

We *can* intentionally take a window of time to focus on our child and make a connection. If we do, it will make a difference, especially with us dads.

A longitudinal study based on seventeen thousand children born in 1958 and followed up at ages seven, eleven, sixteen, twenty-three, and thirty-three reported these findings:

- Children with involved fathers have fewer emotional and behavioral difficulties in adolescence.
- Teens who feel close to their fathers in adolescence go on to have more satisfactory adult marital relationships.
- Girls who have a strong relationship with their fathers during their teen years showed a lack of severe emotional problems as adults.[2]

Other research reports that dads who connect with their children help them deal with teasing and bullies, have success in school, develop healthy body images, and avoid eating disorders.[3] The results remind me of that old TV commercial with the mechanic warning us about regularly changing our car's oil: "You can pay me now or you can pay me later." Clearly, with children, we're all better off making the investments in time to connect "every three thousand miles" rather than waiting until their motor blows up and the fixes are so much more costly.

Think of spending time with your kids now as helping them to be emotionally healthy and having the groundwork for strong marriages. If that's not enough incentive, consider also that you're doing it for the benefit of your future grandchildren.

CALM PARENTS CONNECT

"My parents are *hyper,*" Jason emphasized as he pointed at his dad's foot tapping on my office carpet. "See? They can't sit still. It's always 'Do this' or 'Do that' or 'Come on, get in the car, it's time to go' wherever the heck *they* want to go. They need to chill!" He paused to see their reaction.

After a silence, his mom said, "Jason's right. I agree. We're always on the go. I thought kids liked activity. We don't want them to be bored."

"I'm at a loss," admitted his dad. "Which do they want? Nice things, sports and activities, or less? I'm working hard to pay for this stuff, and I want to know." He looked at his son, then glanced at his wristwatch.

I spoke up. "Every child needs a mom and a dad who are approachable and available, not at all times, but at some time during the day. He needs a parent who listens to his concerns and shows interest in his ideas. A child needs a parent who will take time and doesn't have to swap information in a hurry. He needs parents who are slow to anger and who seldom overreact. Am I on course, Jason?"

"Yeah. There's so much drama in our house. A lot of over-reacting. I do it too."

His mom smiled at his confession. "So what should we do?"

"That's all the time we have for today—that'll be a hundred dollars," I announced. (Not really, just trying to see if you're paying attention.) Actually, I said, "Let me introduce you to an acronym that will help you experience calm and connection. Jason already used the word *chill*." I wrote *CHILL* on my whiteboard. "C stands for Consistent. If we're going to have the kind of secure home that breeds connecting, it needs to be consistent. Inconsistency leads to tension and drama."

"That's us." She let out a deep sigh.

"H is for Halt, which means we will halt our activities in order to connect. It might mean physically stopping whatever we're doing to really tune in to each other. Put the newspaper down, mute the ball game, take off the headphones, whatever. It shows the other persons that they have value and that we respect them."

"There's a lack of respect in our home," said the dad, obviously directing it toward Jason.

"The I is the third quality to CHILL; it reminds us to stay Informed of our child's developmental issues, needs, and desires, and to be informed of his capabilities and circumstances. If we are informed, we'll have reasonable expectations for him."

Jason nodded his head in agreement.

"The first L is Listen. Listen to Jason without interrupting, correcting, or lecturing. The goal isn't to revise his words when he says something wacky. You aren't listening to sharpen his grammar or behavior; you're listening to connect. Remember: listening means *connect, not correct.*"

"We're better at talking than listening," Dad admitted, the edge to his voice having faded.

"And Jason, you can show respect to your parents by listening to them even when you don't agree. That's showing respect."

He bobbed his head.

Dad raised his eyebrows and smiled at Jason.

"And the second L represents Lead by example."

Dad shifted in the couch and rearranged the pillow.

"If we're going to CHILL and not set each other off and over-react, we need to set the pace as parents. Children need calm parents, not stressed-out models of mania. They need to see adults demonstrating behaviors to emulate, including concern for each other, willingness to be humble and ask forgiveness, and acceptance of responsibility without blaming. If you blow it, say, 'I'm sorry, my bad.' We don't have to be perfect, but we do have to be authentic."

> **C**onsistent
> **H**alt
> **I**nformed
> **L**isten and
> **L**ead by example

Our culture has successfully imprinted on our brains that "more is better." You need *more* stuff. You need *more* experiences. Your children require *more* enrichment. It's like we live our lives with a calculator that only has the plus sign; we're constantly *adding* to our lives without subtracting.

After I spoke on this subject in San Diego, a man introduced himself: "We were talking about this at work this week, and about how we're caught up in a culture of 'a little more.' We decided it's not always good. In fact, we now have a saying, 'A little more is the enemy of good.'"

"Explain that to me."

"Sometimes, when we're working, we try to do too much. It starts with the compulsion to do a little more, and it can often risk all the work we've done. Sometimes we need to settle for good, and just say, 'Good enough.'"

"Great point. What was that saying again?"

"A little more is the enemy of good."

"Thanks. An excellent motto. What kind of work are you in?"

"I'm a surgeon."

I became nervous at the mere thought. I wouldn't want a surgeon trying to do too much on me; I want him to do a good job, not a heroic job. I want this guy, the one who'd discovered that *a little more is the enemy of good.*

I'm not saying we should slack off and do sloppy work. I am saying that *more is not always better.*

The Commission on Children at Risk has issued a major report in which it is argued that the loss of connectedness is devastating America's youth:

> The symptoms include major depression, suicide attempts, alcohol abuse, and a wide variety of physical ailments, including asthma, heart disease, irritable bowel syndrome, and ulcers—not to mention crime, delinquency, and dropping out of school. One in five American children are at serious risk of emotional problems. Why? Because they are missing connectedness. Human beings have an inborn need for connections, first with their parents and families, then with larger communities. It is the weakening of the connections between children and their extended families and communities that is producing a virtual epidemic of emotional and behavioral problems.[4]

A hundred years ago, miners used canaries, which have fragile respiratory systems, to alert them to toxic fumes in the mines. Today our most vulnerable systems are in our children . . . and they're gasping for air.

A LEGACY OF CONNECTION

We can do something about our gasping kids. We can't determine or decide every choice they will make, but we *can* actually choose what we will pass on to them. How we parent our children will determine whether in their early years they feel connected or disconnected, bonded or abandoned.

We can pass on a legacy or a lunacy.

We all know what a lunacy is; it's the brokenness, pain, dysfunction, and shame that we might have in our own lives or that we received from our family of origin. But we don't have to hand it down. Because of God's grace, we can be a transitional generation: "The craziness ends here. I'm not going to pass it on. I'll be the last crazy!"

A legacy is something of enduring worth passed on from generation to generation. It is more than a financial inheritance, which our children and grandchildren can blow. This is a spiritual and emotional inheritance that nourishes and guides them long after we're gone.

Have you ever heard a sermon based on the only unnumbered page in the Bible? Look at the blank page(s) between the Old Testament and the New Testament; they carry forward a common theme from the Old Testament to the New. This is the theme of legacy—what gets transmitted from generation to generation. The concept of legacy is biblical.

In graduate school, they taught us about *the principle of first mention*—that the initial biblical introduction of something has special emphasis and sets the template for subsequent references to it. They also taught us about *the principle of last mention*—that the concluding passage of a biblical theme wraps up and conclusively defines it.

> Look ahead: I'm sending Elijah the prophet to clear the way for the Big Day of GOD—the decisive Judgment Day! He will convince parents to look after their children and children to look up to their parents. If they refuse, I'll come and put the land under a curse. (Malachi 4:5–6 THE MESSAGE)

This is a literary metaphor referring to Christ's return and the subsequent Day of Judgment, when God will evaluate each person's eternal status. For those who are in Christ, our individual salvation is guaranteed because we placed our trust in Him; He paid for our sin on the cross. We don't have to worry about that element of judgment.

The Malachi passage warns about a *corporate* and *generational* issue. If parents fail to look after their children and instead turn their hearts away, and if children respond in kind, with dishonor and disrespect, then God will curse the land. Whatever the curse entails, it won't be good—whether sickness, alienation, invasion, terrorism, violence, pestilence, loss of income, and/or natural disasters. God can allow these kinds of calamities to occur by removing His blessing of protection. The universe's natural default setting toward disorder (recall the Second Law of Thermodynamics) would be in full play.

We must respond to the wakeup call. The New International Version says the prophet Elijah's preaching will "turn the hearts of parents to their children" and vice versa. What does this mean?

What does it mean to "turn the hearts toward" (v. 6)? Notice again how Eugene Peterson records it (in *The Message*): "convince parents to *look after* their children and children to look up to their parents." We need to look after our children by caring for them, protecting them, nurturing them, and guiding them, the same way an alert shepherd looks after his sheep. Self-absorption—with projects, schedules, ambitions, worries, hobbies—leads to neglect and even abandonment, robbing us of the time and energy to look after our kids.

Children are to *look up* to their parents, honoring them by listening to them, by responding with obedience, by showing respect, by being teachable, by assuming they can benefit from experience and wisdom. Some lessons for life are best learned from parents; looking up to them enhances our opportunities to learn. Parents don't have to be perfect to be honored—God, in Exodus 20:12, does not say "Honor them if they're perfect." Parenthood carries an intrinsic value that's worthy of honor.

We can avoid a generational curse if we turn our hearts toward one another, if we produce families of love, respect, and honor. Isn't it interesting that God doesn't warn us to turn our hearts toward the folks at church? Or toward the lost, or the homeless, or those in foreign lands?

The real test of priority is family first. As goes the family, so go the church, the community, the state, and the nation. God's priority is the family; that's where we first need to get our hearts right.

THE BLESSING

The best things in life aren't things. You can pass on an inheritance of profound and priceless value to your kids by giving them a biblical blessing. What does God's blessing look like? Well, here's what it's not: wads of money, a sporty car, or a Cancun spring break. *The best gifts to our children come from our example of putting first things first.*

> You shall not make for yourself an idol in the form of anything in heaven above or on the earth beneath or in the waters below. You shall not bow down to them or worship them; for I, the LORD your God, am a jealous God, punishing the children for the sin of the fathers to the third and

fourth generation of those who hate me . . .

STOP!

Anything else that takes first place in our life, even our child, becomes an idol. Only God deserves to be number one. Generational problems—abuse, dysfunction, addiction, compulsions, and the like—get passed on as a result of wrong priorities. Specifically, curses move from generation to generation when we enthrone anyone or anything but God and when we have our hearts turned away from Him and from one another.

> . . . but showing love to a thousand generations of those who love me and keep my commandments. (Exodus 20:4–6)

Did you catch that? I mean, really catch it? Let it soak in. God promises to show love, not to three or four or five generations but a *thousand*! I like to remind parents that even if they came from a cursed family of craziness and brokenness, they don't have to pass it along. They can become the transitional generation if they remember that *the blessing is greater than the curse.* Say it aloud: "The blessing is greater than the curse." That is God's promise. He gave it from the same mouth and the same authority with which He created the universe.

You might be asking, "*How* can I turn my heart toward my kids and bless them?"

Demonstrate to your children their importance to you. Keep pictures of them at your office and with you when you travel. Ask them about their day and ask to see their schoolwork. When you're out of town, call them and let them know you miss them and you want to hear how they are. This has more to do with the little things, done with consistency, than with some grand event.

A parent's focus impacts his children. You can choose a blessing or a curse, depending on your focus. Upon what is your heart set?

Children who grow up in an observant Jewish home often hear the Sh'ma recited. In many of these homes, a child receives several blessings daily from his father. In some Christian homes, a child receives none his entire life.

How have we missed out? We haven't followed the simple plan outlined in Scripture.

> Love the LORD your God with all your heart and with all your soul and with all your strength. These commandments that I give you today are to be upon your hearts. Impress them on your children. Talk about them when you sit at home and when you walk along the road, when you lie down and when you get up. Tie them as symbols on your hands and bind them on your foreheads. Write them on the doorframes of your houses and on your gates. (Deuteronomy 6:5–9)

We demonstrate love best when it consumes us—infiltrating and permeating our heart, our soul, and our strength. This is how God wants us to bless our kids—with a consuming passion for Him. Our faith is contagious! When our children see our all-encompassing love for God, they are most likely to be attracted to our faith.

And it's not just about getting them to Sunday school or making sure they hear good messages in church. It's about naturally working our passion for God into the natural routine of life.

- Eating together at the dining room table
- Taking the dog for a walk together
- Sharing together at bedtime
- Talking together in the morning

We can weave conversations about God and His Word into each of these situations (and many more). Then, in case we temporarily forget, we have reminders around the house, symbols of faith hanging on the walls or by the doors. (Or if we're especially memory-challenged, even tied on our wrists!)

THE LAST CRAZY

"Our fourteen-year-old, Kristy, gives us no respect, and she's really getting a mouth on her," explained Debra.

"I've had it with her. We need to figure out what to do before I regret doing something in anger," admitted Larry.

"What set all of this off?" I asked.

"Well, a couple of nights ago, we had some neighbor friends over for a barbeque. Nothing big, just a get-together on a weeknight. I asked her to get something from the kitchen and she mouthed off to me—'Get your own blankety-blank sauce.' And I went through the roof!"

"Yeah, you did." Debra smiled as she patted Larry's massive forearm.

"I work construction and we don't take lip from nobody, let alone a fourteen-year-old girl. I swore back at her and told her to go to her room."

"She caused all of this drama in front of our friends."

"Were you embarrassed?"

"Yeah, it put a chill on the mood."

"It seems to be getting worse."

"When does she act out?" I queried.

"When we're with friends." Larry looked to Debra for affirmation; she nodded in agreement.

"How often do you get together with friends?"

"About three or four nights during the week we get together

for drinks, dinner, or barbeque. We like to smoke pot on the weekends," Larry said.

"Are you drinking a lot when you get together?"

"Yeah, I guess so. We aren't driving or anything, since it's all neighbors. Everybody just walks home."

"So about three times a week, on school nights, you guys are partying?"

Debra looked at Larry, then to me. "Yeah. Is that a problem?"

I was thankful I'm a trained professional who's learned to not freak out and react when clients say extremely stupid things. I acted unaffected. "Yes, that may have an impact on Kristy's behavior." (Inside I was screaming, *Your kid is normal! She's reacting to your craziness!*) "She's showing disrespect in response to your choices. What might be normal to you isn't acceptable to her."

"We've been partying for twenty years. It does seem normal. In fact, Larry and I met at a party in high school."

"Do your parents have substance-abuse issues?"

Larry looked stunned. "They're all alcoholics. Why?"

"So you grew up with this kind of lifestyle?"

"Both of us did, yeah. We added the weed, but we save it for the weekends, since we both have to work."

"It could be that Kristy is worried. She loves you, sees the mess her grandparents are in, and fears you're headed for the same."

"Is she trying to help or just tick us off? 'Cuz she's sure doing a good job of ticking us off!"

"She could be doing it out of love. Fourteen-year-olds don't have a lot of skills for this kind of thing. They do know how to act out, be defiant, and sass. It could be a cry for attention."

"We know she doesn't approve, but I didn't think this had anything to do with her behavior."

"It does."

"How?"

"She's learning disrespect from you. You want her to be responsible and take care of her body and mind, but she sees you doing the opposite, which she might consider hypocritical. You've also taught her to push the envelope, add drama, and dis the rules."

"Got that right."

"She learned it from you." I looked directly into Larry's eyes. *This will probably be his last appointment, but I have to say it.* "When you break the law by smoking weed, you're teaching your child to disrespect authority—yours."

"I never thought about it that way," he admitted. "No wonder she's so ticked. We need to back it down some. I've been thinking about stopping the pot anyway. What else?"

"Add some structure and routine to your week. She might be feeling that the weeknights are out of control. She'd probably like to come home to a quiet house without guests and eat a meal together, just the family."

"She said that the other day," recalled Debra. "'Why can't we just sit down and have a dinner like a normal family?' We could. It would actually be easier."

"It's better for your body too. You won't wake up feeling groggy or drained."

When Debra asked for additional guidance, I gave them a few pointers and then said good-bye for the day.

———

The next day Debra called. "Tim, I'm at the high school talking with the principal, a counselor, a few teachers, and some parents about the advice you gave us last night. I told them that I want it to be better for Kristy than what I had. I want to be *the last crazy.* They loved the idea and want you to come do a seminar for parents. I've been handing out your flyer, but I thought I should ask you: Do you want twenty more crazy families like ours?"

How about you? Do you want to do better for your child or grandchild? What will you pass on—a lunacy or a legacy?

Your focus as a parent is best spent on the people you love, not on ways to keep the family busy.

DISCUSSION QUESTIONS

Parent to Parent

1. What do you think about this statement: "We often restore our strength in the company of our friends"?
2. What is the difference between building a relationship and growing one?
3. Review CHILL. What are some ways to grow these qualities as a parent?
4. How can we know when "enough is enough"?
5. In what ways could a blessing demonstrate to our children that we are putting first things first?

Parent and Child

1. Describe a time when hanging with your friends actually recharged your energy.

2. Do you know (or know of) some overscheduled kids? What are their lives like?
3. Parents are to be honored and kids are to be loved; how does this look on an average day?

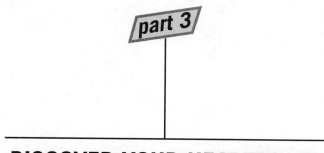

DISCOVER YOUR HEARTPRINT

CHAPTER SIX

The Four Heartprints

Imagine that a family of four is out together for a walk.

Randy, the father, is aiming for exercise. He quickly strides ahead. He'd rather be running.

His wife, Wanda, likes to pace more slowly, enjoying the fresh air and the blossoms. She takes her time and listens to their six-year-old son, Craig, who stops to look at "rollie-pollies" and pick up a discarded matchstick: "Look, Mommy, I found some litter."

Randy turns back and sees Craig kneeling on the sidewalk, looking for more insects and trash. He halts his fevered gait and places both hands on his hips. "C'mon, let's go!"

Twelve-year-old Bracey stops to see what's consuming her little brother; she rubs his hair, then sprints ahead. As she passes her father she chides, "Let's pick it up, ol' man!"

Four different people. Four different paces. And a recipe for conflict . . . even though all they're doing is sharing a walk!

Sound familiar?

Most families have members with different heartbeats. *Your heartbeat is the pace that you prefer for life.* As with walking, people like to move at various speeds, each stride having its strengths and weaknesses. There isn't one right pulse for everyone; in fact, your heartbeat is unique to you, like a thumbprint. No one else's heartbeat is quite like yours—it's your *heartprint.*

Note the four heartprints in the story:

Randy *Runner* wants to keep things moving, to fill each day with activity, to take a quick stride through the whole of life.

Wanda *Walker* likes to maintain a slow and steady pace, and she can't personally relate to a persistent need for going fast; she's content to carry on a conversation and enjoy the surroundings.

Craig *Cruiser* is unhurried and hates to be rushed—he's afraid he'll miss something. Craig's ambulating pace and obsession for details often frustrate Randy Runner, who worries it will keep him from accomplishing his goals.

Bracey *Biathlete* is a combination of Randy and Craig: She aims to go fast and beat her dad, but then she also wants short periods of rest—it's a varied approach. Ever seen a biathlete in the Winter Olympics? She cross-country skis at a blistering pace, and then, when she reaches a shooting area, stops, pulls a rifle off her back, controls her breathing, and fires calmly at her target. Fast, then slow.

Your family also is some combination of these four types.

How do we find a balance? How do we discover the ideal pace for our family when we're all at different speeds?

With an understanding and embracing of others' heartprints, we can discover the pace that includes every family member. With sensitivity, investigation, and creativity, you can discover the perfect pulse for *your* family!

I'm not saying all families need to slow down—some function well together at a fast pace. What I'm saying is *know why you do what you do.* Don't keep adding activities to your schedule just because you can. That you can doesn't mean you should.

YOUR CHILD IS BENT

One of the most quoted scriptures on parenting is Proverbs 22:6:

Point your kids in the right direction—
when they're old they won't be lost. (THE MESSAGE)

Every boy and girl is created with a unique God-given design. The words *right direction* or *the way* come from a Hebrew term that means "the natural bent." The Creator has designed the personality, intellect, and heartprint of every human being. He has purposefully made your child with these propensities; it's our job to discover his or her natural bent and affirm it as God's handiwork. Remember the saying "God don't make no junk!"

I like to compare a child's natural bent to the curves of a tree trunk. An oak is destined to be an oak before the seedling pops above the soil. Its genetic properties are determined; it's not going to turn into a squash, for God has designed it to be an oak. Even so, as that oak matures, the environment to some extent will shape it with wind, rain, soil, and other properties.

The same is true of your child: God has purposely created him with a particular nature; you must shape, mold, guide, and affirm that design. This is a biblical balancing of the classic "nature vs. nurture" debate. We nurture what God has created; we discover our child's bent—tendencies, interests, giftedness, and passions—then embrace and develop them. When we do, we partner with God in fulfilling His purposes for our child. As the child grows older, he will know the way he was meant to walk.

ALL IN THE BOAT

Jeanne yelled from the kitchen to her twelve-year-old son. "Ryan, your karate studio just called—you don't have class today. The instructor is sick!"

"*Yeah*, free day!" he cheered as he bounded down the stairs. "No soccer, no tutoring, no drama. Now I can play!" He grabbed his basketball and went out the front door to shoot hoops on the driveway.

"That's the most excited I have seen him in weeks," Jeanne confided to me later. "Frankly, I'm concerned because he seems so withdrawn."

"Why's that?" I asked.

"Because he doesn't enjoy all the activity like his brother and sister. He'd rather play by himself, or sometimes with the neighborhood kids. He seems content just to shoot baskets. Is there something wrong?"

"Maybe he's a Cruiser in a family of Runners."

"What?"

"A Cruiser likes to take things slow. Ryan is more easygoing than you or your husband. In fact, he probably likes to take things easier than anyone else in the family. Correct?"

"Absolutely. I thought I was helping him by signing him up for activities; maybe I pushed him too far?"

"He might resent being so busy. You may have picked a pace that's right for others but too much activity for Ryan. There are four kinds of paces. I call them *heartprints:* Cruisers, Walkers, Runners, and Biathletes. He's probably a Cruiser. They like a drawn-out cadence that helps assure they'll do things right."

"Have you been spying on us? That's exactly what he does. It bugs Mike and it bugs me. We're trying to get ready to go for the weekend, and Ryan's organizing his video games chronologically on the game room bookshelf!"

"Cruisers are concerned with order and quality. Their motto is 'Don't rush—do it right.' In a word, they're compliant. They will follow the rules, keep things in order, move slowly, and know where everything is."

"That's for sure. He's the only one in the family that doesn't lose stuff. But it's annoying sometimes because he's so slow."

"He probably struggles with you going so fast. He may not feel included or valued."

"No wonder he's been acting up lately. What can we do?"

"The misbehavior is often a clue; we call it *acting out*. Kids don't always tell us what's wrong through their talk; they show us something is wrong by their behavior. You know, misbehaving to catch our attention."

"That's what's been happening. Do I have to cancel all his activities?"

"Now that he's twelve, ask him how many activities he wants to do after school. Some kids benefit more from free play than organized activity."

"Think of all the money I could have saved," Jeanne joked.

"I know. But ask him if he'd like to cut it down to one activity, then have him choose."

"We're going to the lake this weekend. What should we do about that? He loves to wakeboard. Is going to the lake helping or is that too much?"

"I'm guessing he's fine with it—when he's wakeboarding, he can control the speed of the boat with a thumbs up or down. It's empowering to him."

"Now that I think about it, Ryan does like to go slow. We've even called him the old-man cruiser!"

"So try this: With everybody in the boat, take a little time just to downshift. After everyone has wakeboarded, have Mike cruise around at a very slow pace. Just enjoy the beauty of the lake and each other. No rush. No performance. No competition. Just relaxing together as a family."

"Is that where the phrase 'We're all in the same boat' comes from?"

"I don't know, but it fits. You *are* all in the same boat, showing consideration for each other's heartprints. This will make Ryan feel valued and wanted. There will be plenty of time to race around and do the flashy stuff; make sure you take time to include every family member. Think inclusively, and affirm each person's heartprint."

"In a way, we've discriminated against Ryan. We are all so manic and he's not. No wonder. I'll give it a try."

―――――――――

The following week I asked Jeanne, "How was the lake?"

"It went very well. We did what you suggested and cruised around at sunset. It was beautiful. We saw deer, fish, an eagle, and some caves we'd never seen."

"Because you were going slower?"

"Yup. Ryan loved it. We only did it for twenty minutes, because the rest of us were getting fidgety. But it seemed to mean a lot to him."

"How was his behavior?"

"He was great. I think that just showing an understanding of his preferences kept him from creating a scene."

"How was it for you?"

"It was a helpful lesson for me also. I'm always so driven. I need to learn to downshift sometimes and vary the speed."

"Even runners need rest."

"Yeah, they do!"

CRUISERS

Cruisers tend to be guarded, vigilant, and reserved. Typically, a Cruiser is not known as a party animal but rather as an industrious worker. He likes to have control of the situation and feels out of control if things are going too fast. A Cruiser is likely to slow down when he feels stress because he doesn't want to make mistakes. If he's rushed and makes errors, he's likely to feel afraid and discouraged. A Cruiser becomes irritated when he can't regulate his environment or produce quality. *Cruisers build to last.*

Cruisers want life to be predictable—no interruptions, no challenges to the routine, and nobody intruding on their project. They like to do things by the book. They are compliant, with a passion for detail; they are persistent; some become perfectionists. Because they're analytical, Cruisers tend to be skilled at critically examining all sides before making a decision. Cruisers are willing to say no when they see problems; they aren't too worried about the reactions of others. They just want to get the job done, and they want to get it done right—the first time.

WALKERS

Our culture is hostile to relaxing walks. Bikes, scooters, skateboards, motorcycles, cars, trucks, planes, trains, and even buses get us around much faster. I saw a rare sight the other day: an entire family out for a walk. Father, mother, son, and daughter enjoying the magnificence of a warm California winter day, just before sunset. I wanted to take a picture!

Isn't it sad that such a scene is so rare?

You may have a child who would love to take a walk with her family. You might have a child who would enjoy a family Sabbath celebration every weekend. You may have a spouse who is desperate for time to pause, break, and breathe. It might even be you.

Not everyone likes a fast pace. *Some like to live life slow and steady.*

Walkers usually prefer to move a bit more quickly than Cruisers. While Cruisers are content with a deliberate pace—one that allows them time to soak in the details, *Walkers like to maintain a steady progress forward.* They aren't in a hurry, but they're not so concerned with details as Cruisers. Walkers like to walk and talk without being breathless: "A steady pace wins the race." Walkers aren't going to be speedy, but they will be steady.

You might be a Walker if:

- You enjoy walking outdoors and hate the noise and hubbub of a gym.
- You pride yourself on your consistency.
- You dislike change and enjoy routine.
- You've maintained friendships for years.
- You're a peacemaker and prefer to avoid conflict.
- You love receiving approval for a job well done.
- Others have affirmed your loyalty and patience.

If you feel perplexed and don't know what to do, go on a long walk with a Walker—they're sympathetic listeners. I personally like to surround myself with Walkers; they're faithful, patient, and willing to wait for something.

When you assign a task to a Walker, she will continue to work on that task as long as needed; she wants to please you and be seen as a stable, reliable friend. Walkers also are wonderful team players because they don't have to have the ball—they've learned to share, and they truly care about others. They hate it when people are excluded and will labor to make everyone feel accepted.

RUNNERS

Runners like to fill each day with the most endeavors they can possibly squeeze in. They like to say yes, and they have a tendency to overcommit. They like the excitement of a rapid pulse, and they prefer to run in herds—that way there are plenty of people to converse and be active with. The Runner's motto is, "Yes! Why not?"

You might be a Runner if:

- You've been labeled "Type A."
- You schedule full days so you won't miss out on anything or anybody.
- Everyone is your friend.

- You might not be concerned with details, but you can "work the room."
- You're the life of the party.
- You're creative and energetic.
- In a word, you're *involved*.

Runners like to live life at warp speed. They like to take risks and sip their water from a fire hose. If you're a Cruiser parent with a Runner child, you may suspect that he's hyperactive. If you're a Walker parent with a Runner child, you may suspect that his inconsistencies and tendency to avoid details will cause problems. If you're a Runner parent with a Runner child, you may both be so busy that you don't feel very connected.

BIATHLETES

The actual biathletes are hearty competitors: they ski furiously for several kilometers, stop at a target range, pull a lightweight rifle from a sling, catch their breath, and fire several accurate shots . . . then repeat the process.

Biathletes have to be skilled at both skiing and shooting—moving at a frenzied pace *and* firing with skilled marksmanship. When the rest of us would be bent over and huffing, these remarkable specimens have learned how to go and stop, go and stop, very quickly and very smoothly.

The Biathlete's heartprint likes lots of variety between very fast and slow. Biathletes are extremely competitive and strategic. They have to carefully pace themselves so they won't be too winded when it comes to the slowdown. They generally reject routine in favor of adventure and challenges. Biathletes are bold and self-reliant explorers.

The Biathlete's motto? "Variety is the spice of life." Biathletes are often leaders—decisive, daring, and directive. They like to give orders but not receive them; they'd rather be in charge. Many entrepreneurs are biathletes—unafraid of risk, willing to try new things, often needing new challenges to keep them from being bored.

Biathletes are assertive, action oriented, and motivated—sometimes so motivated that they mow over others in the process. They also can tend toward being aggressive and insensitive to the needs and frailties of others who appear to be weak.

Biathletes get disillusioned with the steady pace that pleases Cruisers and Walkers. They want to vary intense activity with non-activity. (Go, then stop.)

You may be a Biathlete if:

- You like to control things.
- You hate being bored but love variety.
- You're ambitious and want to direct others.
- You can make decisions easily.
- You're excited and energized when facing challenges.
- After an intense time you want to shut down, rest, and be left alone.

In the next four chapters we'll discuss how to parent Cruisers, Walkers, Runners, and Biathletes.

DISCUSSION QUESTIONS

Parent to Parent

1. With which heartprint do you most closely identify: Cruiser, Walker, Runner, or Biathlete?
2. What heartprint do your other family members have? How do you know?
3. What do you think of this advice: "Don't keep adding

activities to your schedule just because you can. That you can doesn't mean you should."

4. How can you discover the bent of your child?
5. Considering your heartprint, describe the perfect day for you.

Parent and Child

1. Describe the qualities of the four heartprints to your child. Ask, "Do you know someone like this?" and "Which one seems most like you?"
2. Ask your child some "would you rather" questions. This can be helpful in determining his or her bent. Example: Would you rather ride a bike or walk; drive a limo or a monster truck; be a spectator or a player on the field; go to a movie or be in a movie?

CHAPTER SEVEN

Parenting a Cruiser

If you think your child may be a Cruiser, try having him watch TV. I know, not what you'd expect from a parenting guy. But not any TV, mind you—have your child watch *Jeopardy*.

Why?

Because the most obvious Cruiser in pop culture is Ken Jennings, the brilliant computer programmer from Utah who won two and a half million dollars on the show. To keep his winnings going, he answered 2,700 questions correctly! He appeared in seventy-four consecutive episodes. In several categories he demonstrated topical mastery by achieving a run (consecutively answering all the questions correctly) while his competitors watched with mouths agape.

Getting it right.

A Cruiser's dream come true.

Accuracy is crucial for a Cruiser, whether he's four or forty. Cruisers are God's little engineers. When a Cruiser sets his mind to a task, he'll perform it correctly and he'll complete it. He will carefully plan, develop lots of blueprints, consider the variables, produce a timeline, do all due diligence, stick to the schedule . . . and all in a clean and tidy fashion.

You may be a Cruiser if you don't like living at breakneck velocity. If you've been called particular, choosy, or obsessive because you won't rush to complete a task, you could be a Cruiser.

You might be a Cruiser if:

- Your shirts are arranged by color in your closet.
- Your tools are organized on a pegboard above your clean workbench.
- Your idea of a fun evening is finding a thick historical novel at the library and reading it at home.
- You aren't impressed with speed but with a job well done.
- You make things that are built to last.

CRUISER KIDS

If you have a Cruiser child, expect her to ask a lot of questions; she's prone to be inquisitive, wanting to know how things work and relate to each other. She'll persistently stick with something until she's figured it out or completed it. A Cruiser strives to master tasks and topics, and you can frustrate her by stopping in the middle of a game or a project. She doesn't like leaving *anything* half done—her goals include resolution and excellence.

Cruisers are focused: While they may start only one or two projects a year, they'll see them through. Cruisers love to make lists, which help them activate their prodigious mental database—complete with details, facts, and experiences (all categorized and cross-filed).

Cruisers prefer a deliberate stream of activity and an unhurried process; their heartprint accommodates their analytical bent. For a preschool Cruiser, make a chore chart with icons or pictures for two or three tasks you want him to complete every day: picking up toys; telling you when he needs to be changed; informing you when he's ready to use the toilet; taking a nap; behaving in the store; being reasonably quiet in the car; and so on. Buy some stickers. Each time he does his job, give him a sticker to place on the chart—he will love seeing the progression of stickers.

Cruisers tend to think in black and white, so highlight truth and contrast right and wrong. Make sure that in your habits you are consistent and predictable: Don't vary the routine without warning him. Cruisers like to know what's coming and when, because they feel secure when they know the routine. Encourage him with stick-on notes, and make sure he has the tools he needs for list-making and organization.

Cruisers love schedules and agendas. Ask your elementary-age Cruiser child to help you make the grocery list or Saturday's schedule of activities: "My soccer game at nine; sister's at eleven; lunch at McDonald's; yard work as a family; barbeque hamburgers; rent a family video for the evening."

As they mature, help them make sense of their faith. Take time to explore specific answers to their questions. Help them discover reasons for their beliefs. Regard doubts as opportunities to explore rather than as indications of instability or lack of trust.

DISCUSSION QUESTIONS

Parent to Parent

1. Why do you think *getting it right* is so important to a Cruiser child?
2. What are some of the benefits of having a Cruiser child? What are some of the unique challenges?
3. What do you think about the advice to not rush a Cruiser child?
4. Why is it important to be sensitive to the slower-placed heartprint of your Cruiser child?

Parent and Child

1. Do one of the suggested projects, like a chore chart or a weekend schedule, and discuss it with your child. Ask for

feedback: "What do you think of it?" "Do you like the idea?" "How will it help?" "What could make it better?"

2. Encourage him to talk about his doubts and worries. Sometimes he'll be more open to talking about them after you read him a story that helps him relate to the doubts and worries of a character.

CHAPTER EIGHT

Parenting a Walker

I've learned a lot from my dog.

My wife bought me a golden retriever puppy for our anniversary this year. Suzanne dubbed her "Annie," short for *anniversary*.

It was a mixed bag. I returned from a trip to find my wife gone (obviously hiding out) and a six-week-old bundle of blond fur in our home. My first reaction was agitation. *We finally got rid of the kids and have an empty nest—and she brings home a PUPPY?!*

I got over it in about four minutes. Now I walk her every day. Otherwise she destroys my backyard. (My puppy, not my wife.)

Here's some of what I've learned on our walks:

- Few people walk anymore. Most speed around in their cars.
- Most people in cars aren't smiling.
- Almost all walkers and dog owners smile, wave, or say hello.
- Walking lends the freedom to stop and chat, look at a squirrel, or sniff the roses.
- Many homes are empty (dark) at dinnertime; I wonder where the people are.
- The two parks within two blocks of our home are empty most of the time.
- Most people in our neighborhood don't know their neighbors.
- I'm getting to know some of the neighborhood kids, possibly because I'm one of the few adults they see who has time to talk.

- Everyone who can should get a dog; everyone who can should walk.

People are feeling rushed and disconnected. There seems to be an ache in our culture for belonging. For all the talk about "community," most of us are still missing it.

Especially the Walkers.

An adult Walker is the poster child for "The Good Neighbor." This heartprint has a passion for community; Walkers are loyal and considerate, the people who thrive on the thirty-fourth annual Memorial Day barbeque—anything predictable, fun, conflict-free, and unhurried. Walkers don't like to be pressured. A Walker is rarely in a hurry—she likes to be patient, thoughtful, and understanding, and she is eager to please.

WALKER KIDS

Walkers thrive on relational responsibilities—that's why they're Walkers. It's not about getting the job done rapidly; it's about staying connected and being consistent along the way.

If your child is a Walker, help her to learn that it's okay to say no. Because she's a people-pleaser, she may otherwise constantly default to saying yes. Walkers deeply care about others, and they want everyone to be included; for example, it will be difficult for your Walker child to limit her birthday party invitation list—she wants everyone to come. Walkers are extremely sensitive and can be easily hurt; even though they're strong, they're responsive to how others treat them. They love the regularity and anticipation of rituals, like "The Good Morning Song" they sing first thing at preschool, or the way Mommy tucks them into bed every night.

Preschool Walkers can sense tension in the home even before they talk about it—they tend to be remarkably perceptive with their senses. Help them avoid taking on concerns and issues that are for Mom and Dad. Demonstrate consistent love and care for them by reading or singing to them each night before bed. Make sure they feel safe, cared for, and close to you.

Walkers are open to taking care of others. Think of ways your Walker child can utilize this bent: draw a picture for Grandma, help bake cookies for a neighbor, give some of her baby toys to charity, etc.

Elementary-age Walkers are expanding their relational skills at school, and how their friends respond to them is of great significance. Help them develop kindness and humility, take responsibility, say "I'm sorry," avoid cliquishness or exclusivity, and defend someone who's been treated badly.

Because they perceive that they're easily wounded, teenage Walkers can be anxious about conflict, real or imagined. They might be likely to take on stress or worry that doesn't belong to them. Help them develop and then stick to their boundaries. Assist them in developing personal beliefs and values without compromising to be popular or cool. Affirm their role as an integral team player; applaud their loyalty. Through their patience, Walkers learn from the mistakes of others (usually Runners). When you see that your Walker child is tentative or hesitant to try something that she really wants to undertake, you can assist her in receiving the courage to go for it with a "Why not?" nudge.

BUILDING AN ENVIRONMENT FOR WALKERS

Since Walkers embrace routine, one way of creating the right home environment for your Walker child is to have regular family traditions that affirm and soothe her. This includes the practice of passing down stories, beliefs, and customs from one generation to the next in order to establish and reinforce a strong sense of identity. Family traditions strengthen the notion that *our family is safe and reliable;* they illustrate who we are and what's important to us.

For Walkers, family traditions involve certainty, preparation, anticipation, and celebration. Involve your Walker child in planning and facilitating family traditions with the following guidelines of a "Tradition Planner":

1. What stories, beliefs, or customs might develop fun and meaningful tradition in our family?
2. How has a previous generation passed these on to us? How important were these to them? What values or beliefs or customs did not get passed along?
3. Brainstorm a few ways to model or teach some of our most important values and beliefs.
4. Choose one of the ideas listed above and develop a new family tradition.
5. What do we hope to accomplish with this new tradition? How often will we celebrate it? Who's in charge? What resources will we need?[1]

We live in a hurried and transient culture, but the practice of traditions gives our children stability, dependability, and shared memories. These three qualities help people feel connected in relationship and community. This is critical in a rootless society. Traditions, by their very nature, are boundaries: "This is the way we do it. We don't do it that way." Predictable traditions increase our children's sense of personal security because they define a place to stand without being too rigid.[2]

WALK WITH GOD

We are created in God's image. God is more than spirit; He is a person who can know and be known. God has mind, will, and emotion, elements of personhood He also bestowed upon us—we can think, we can decide, and we can feel. Traditions are important because they validate each of these: There is a divine purpose to thinking, deciding, and feeling, for they are reflections of the person of God.

In a culture that largely advocates an impersonal universe and the macroevolution of humans through random chance, it's important that we reinforce the value of life and respect for humans as designed by God in His image. The basic purpose of family traditions is to establish, clarify, and reinforce this in the home.

People of faith have the potential for a strong sense of belonging. Again, we live in a culture desperate for community. We rejoice in connections with family, the community of faith, and the creation of God.

Learn from the Walkers. Take your children to the ocean; let them see the beauty and power of the Creator as you walk along the shore. Take them to a fresh field of wild flowers to breathe in the natural God-given fragrance. Take them to an art museum; let them see the intricate talent of an Impressionist emulating the Master. Take them to a symphony to hear a hundred instruments playing in concert, each contributing in its unique way. Such experiences help children comprehend how we are made in God's likeness. We are people with creativity. We are people of worth.

When we slow down, take our child's hand, and go out on a walk with her—just for fun—we affirm her personhood, we demonstrate that we belong in this world, that we have a place in it, and that we will walk with her to help her discover it.

DISCUSSION QUESTIONS
Parent to Parent

1. Describe a difficult family time that turned out to be different from your intentions.

2. Discuss this concept: *Building a solid, healthy family takes work.* What are some of the elements of a solid foundation?
3. Is the essence of childhood endangered in today's world? Why or why not?
4. Compare and contrast a Cruiser child with a Walker child. What could you do if you had one of each?
5. How do family traditions affirm and include the Walker in your family?

Parent and Child

1. Discuss the qualities of a Cruiser and a Walker with your kids. Ask, "Do these sound like you or more like another family member?"
2. Ask, "What's your favorite family tradition?" "Why do you like it?" "Are there other traditions you'd like for us to celebrate?"
3. Ask your child which of these he or she would like to do:
   • Take a walk at the beach
   • Look at wild flowers
   • Climb a mountain
   • Go to an art museum
   • Go to a concert
   • Ride bikes
   Then try to schedule time to do it!

CHAPTER NINE

Parenting a Runner

You know what it's like to be a parent of preschoolers. Serving countless sippy cups of "shoosh" (juice); wiping up the sticky mess from the was-clean-thirty-minutes-ago kitchen floor; smelling foulness and discovering dog poop caked under your three-year-old's shoes (the same ones in which she's been running through the house); extricating melted crayons embedded in the new living room carpet; cleaning the bathroom around the toilet because your son's aim isn't quite developed; changing your daughter's diaper for the tenth time in one day. *(How can she generate so much?)*

I used to fantasize about escaping the mayhem to the serene ocean, where I'd be surfing ten-foot waves, fighting the current, and keeping an eye out for sharks. Now *that's* relaxing! Actually, what's sad is that my duty as Diaper Daddy usually consisted of only four hours a week while Suzanne had a break from the little tormentors. She took care of them during their other hundred and forty weekly waking hours.

In spite of the challenges, I've come to realize that there's no more meaningful, revolutionary mission than rearing a child. We tend to think it's the media, celebrities, politicians, and peers who hold all the power, but their influence is minuscule compared to a mom's or dad's—those hearty souls who are birthing, raising, and shaping members of the next generation. Even so, sometimes it's hard to keep up, especially if your child is a Runner.

RUNNING CRAZY

As we've seen, Runners live fast. In contrast to Walkers, who like a steady pace and consistency, Runners like activity and stimulation—they'd rather talk than listen. They aren't afraid to take risks—eliminating all risk from your Runner's life would frustrate him. Instead, your mission is to help him discover how to evaluate and gauge risk on his own.

If you have a Runner child, you can help him by prioritizing and planning. Not everything is important—he doesn't have to do *every* activity. Also, don't buy him a detailed model he has to build by following 152 steps. When it comes to gifts for young Runners, buy building blocks, an erector set, or watercolors. Runners are creative and expressive; pragmatic, wordy instructions are *boring*. Runners are innovative, preferring to create and shape things in ways that express them uniquely.

As with a Walker, you may need to help your Runner child learn to say no. While Walkers say yes to everything because they want to please everyone, Runners say yes too much because they want to do everything, thereby pleasing themselves.

Help your Runner child develop checklists or reminders to help him deal with details he's likely to overlook. Use calendars, memos posted on the door or mirror, assignment notebooks, and computer-based planners to help prompt his memory.

Sometimes it helps to limit a socially active Runner's engagements. For instance, say: "You can do one thing after school, one on Saturday, and one on Sunday. You can't spend the night at Jason's on Friday, go to the soccer game on Saturday afternoon, spend Saturday night at the movies with your friends, *and* go to the swap meet with Brandon on Sunday afternoon. Which will you give up?"

Occasionally you'll meet a task-oriented adult Runner who

doesn't much like people but will put up with them so he can experience lots of activity and not get bored as he works through his eighteen-hour day. And, once again, if a family has two or more Runners, they can be so busy that they rarely connect. Their heartprint usually sets the pace for others who'd prefer to take things a little more slowly; Runners can look condescendingly on Cruisers and Walkers, looking down on the different (read: slower) pace. Runners need to avoid believing they are more important than others for having so much to do and so many people to see; they must learn to make accommodations for slower-paced family members.

Recently, I shared this concept with a Runner executive who was complaining about the mess and chaos of his home. He couldn't figure out why his wife couldn't corral the two preschool menaces and have the place in order when he arrived home at six-thirty.

"She doesn't work. Why does it have to be a zoo?"

I asked him to shift gears as he went home, to acknowledge that he was crossing the border from the culture of work to the culture of home. We discussed the contrasts, and I advised, "When you get to one mile away from home, get off your cell phone and start thinking about the culture you're entering. It may seem foreign, confusing, and messy, but it's where your wife has been all day—*The Toddler Zone*. Adjust your expectations and then enter the home prepared to adjust to the different environment."

A few weeks later he reported, "I have a marker one mile from my house and it really works. I get off the phone and spend the last few minutes thinking about and praying for my wife. I used to show up on the driveway and have a kid hanging on each leg while I was still talking on the phone. That seemed to agitate everyone, including me. Now I can cross the border and focus in on my kids and my wife."

It's important that we do our best at home; home needs and deserves more than our leftover energy, passion, and time.

In a comprehensive investigation of family and family values in America by Massachusetts Mutual Life Insurance Company, it was determined from the twelve hundred participants that *"Family is the central element in the lives of most Americans."* The report's conclusion echoes the familiar refrain of "Family First!"

We live in a family-centered society. At a personal level, family is the source of Americans' greatest joys and most significant worries. At a societal level, Americans locate the root causes of our most pressing social problems in the family. The family is the base for caring and nurturing. It is also the place where values are taught and learned. Disrupting either of these functions can produce individuals and societies with serious pathologies.[1]

We make time for who and what is important to us. If family matters, we will carve out time from our demanding schedules to make time for our family . . . even if we're Runners.

THE ROAD LESS TRAVELED

I watched a famous actress on *Oprah* this week. She used to be on the cover of all of the magazines and tabloids, all of the TV entertainment shows. She was everywhere. Oprah asked, "How was that for you?"

"It was okay for a while, but I got tired of it. I finally got over myself and wanted to move on."

"Having a child helped?"

"Yes, it did. It helped me get over myself. Those things pale in comparison. After losing my dad, I realize how important family is. I want to be there for my daughter."

Even high-profile entertainers recognize that their greatest role may be the one they play as Mommy.

Parents impact history—one child at a time.

Remember: If your child is a Runner, she's going to want a high level of activity at a fast pace. You may find it difficult to keep up; however, at least some of the time, join her in her speedy world. At first it may seem like a whirlwind to you, but she needs your involvement and will appreciate your company. Even Runners, with all their frenetic activity, feel connected when a parent is willing to join them on the express-lane highway. It's all about connecting—even at a swift pace.

DISCUSSION QUESTIONS

Parent to Parent

1. In what ways has having a child changed you?
2. What are some practical ways to prioritize planning in choosing your Runner child's activities?
3. Are you a Runner? What characteristics do you see in yourself that tell you yes or no?
4. Discuss how much risk is healthy and when risk is not healthy.
5. How can we be sure we're having more impact on our kids than the media figures they watch and listen to?

Parent and Child

1. Ask, "What are some things that you like to do faster than I prefer?"

2. Discuss and contrast the qualities of Cruisers, Walkers, and Runners with your child. Ask, "Who do we know that fits each of these kinds of people?"
3. Discuss these questions: "How much is too much? How will we know when you have too many activities in your life? What are the signs of overload?"

CHAPTER TEN
Parenting a Biathlete

About twenty years (and twenty pounds) ago, I used to cross-country ski through the snow-frocked Sierras, gliding through pristine meadows, sounds coming only from skis shushing along in the freshly fallen snow. There was something magical about being alone on a fresh white carpet—being the first to lay down tracks. When I paused to catch my breath, I inhaled the splendor of the towering redwoods, sentinels of the forest for hundreds of years. I often spotted deer searching for tidbits of vegetation under the frozen mantle. The evergreens cast fragrant aromas as a breeze descended lightly from the peaks.

It was scintillating. It was refreshing. It was healing.

I needed a break from the hubbub in the valley. I needed respite from the noise, the concrete, the freeways, the clanging beeps of technology, the incessant demands of people. I needed to be alone.

I needed the quiet, to hear just the pounding of my own heart as I ascended the knoll before me.

Have you heard the term "cocooning"? This is the concept of hiding out in your home and recharging for the next day or week. We keep such a rapid pace that at the end of the day we often isolate ourselves in our "cocoon with a mortgage." We don't have the energy to go out—we're spent, devoid of vigor to connect with others. Earlier I mentioned my contribution to the increasing surge in the sale of home theaters: big-screen TVs, surround sound, and recliners provide the theater experience in our own homes. We're too exhausted even to go to the movies!

I've also noticed that it's becoming more and more difficult to recruit volunteers for charitable causes on the weekends. Most of us would rather cocoon, and we're able to justify our bipolar schedules by reasoning *I've been so busy all week that I must have the weekend for myself. I need to recharge.*

The *charge and halt* approach can have a severely negative impact on our health.

> Growing amongst Americans is a common illness called "leisure sickness." This malady manifests itself in several forms, such as flu-like symptoms, headache, sore throat, and muscle aches. Essentially, our bodies and emotions are so stressed out during the week that in the evenings and particularly weekends we fall apart. The only remedy for this social fever is a change in lifestyle.[1]

I've fallen victim to leisure sickness. After a week of writing, speaking, traveling, and working with clients, I'm ready to hole up at home. Again, we have a media room (and I love it).

Now, be quiet and hand me the remote!

Sometimes it's all Suzanne and I can do to get to the grocery store to seize our rations of chips, sodas, and nuts to get us through a Saturday and Sunday of watching home-improvement shows, sports, and *CSI* as we pop ibuprofen and lounge on ice-packs. I'm fascinated with the concept of *leisure sickness,* because honestly, I seem to be living it on many weekends.

Consider that when we push all week, then pull the plug on the weekend, we're buying into some assumptions that keep us trapped in the jam-n-slam routine:

- "Everyone is living this way."
- "I don't have any other choice."

- "Successful people are always busy."
- "I have to do this to pay for my lifestyle."
- "It's going to slow down soon—this is just a phase."

Any of these sound familiar?

Many people reason that *The more money I have, the less stress I'll have, and I'll be able to relax.* By contrast, both studies and my observation show that with increased resources comes increased complexity, not simplicity. The ones who have more actually have more with which to destroy themselves.[2]

DOWNSIZING IN THE SUBURBS

Gary had a beautiful home in a ritzy neighborhood. The house was forty-five minutes from the office, an hour if there was traffic (and there always was). He enjoyed living in the prestigious zip code, but it became a financial challenge, with both he and his wife working insane hours to compensate. When he realized it was beginning to have a negative effect on their marriage and their child, he asked me for advice.

"Would you consider selling your house and moving to a more affordable neighborhood, closer to the office, so you both wouldn't have to work so hard?"

He winced at the idea. "I'll think about it. But we'd be giving up a lot."

"You might be already."

He discussed it with his wife and surprisingly she approved. They sold their house and bought a more affordable one, five minutes from work. With a smile on his face and a sparkle emanating from his well-rested eyes, he said, "Without that commute I have ten more hours a week! My marriage is better and I have time to relax with my son. Last night we were playing catch in the front yard at five-thirty.

"My wife loves not working. She's enjoying gardening and cooking. We don't eat out as much, so we're healthier and have lost weight. I was even able to get a promotion because I'm so close to the office. I'd turned it down earlier because I didn't want the extra responsibility on top of the commute, but now, if they need me to come in, I say, 'Call me, and I'll come—I'm only five minutes away.' I've only had to do it twice, but the thought that I'm available helps. So I have more time and more money, and I am working less. Thanks!"

Gary's situation isn't rare. According to Harvard University's Robert Putnam, in his bestselling book *Bowling Alone,* the average American family engages in thirteen automobile commutes a day! Most commuters spend seventy-two minutes alone in the car. Putnam suggests that for every ten minutes you spend in your car, you reduce your time for relationships (*social capital*) by 10 percent.[3]

We only have so much flextime; if we're spending it alone in the car, we're going into relational debt. Even if others surround us we're very much alone, enduring *crowded loneliness.*

The last several decades have witnessed a striking diminution of regular contacts with our friends and neighbors. We spend less time in conversation over meals, we exchange visits less often, we engage less often in leisure activities that encourage casual social interaction, we spend more time watching and less time doing. We know our neighbors less well, and we see old friends less often.[4]

THE *JAM-N-SLAMMERS*

All of this notwithstanding, a lifestyle of breaking the sound barrier and then collapsing isn't simply a phenomenon among harried suburbanites; it's one of the four heartprints. We've examined the Cruisers, the Walkers, and the Runners; now let's look at the Biathletes.

Recall that actual biathletes are competitors who cross-country ski over hills and through forests, then stop every so often to shoot at a tiny target across the meadow. Their endurance and control are incredible; they are mastering the variety of alternating "very fast" with "almost completely stopped."

If you have a Biathlete child, you might want to give him a challenge or a goal, like "See if you can pick up all these toys in five minutes. Ready, go!"

Let your Biathlete take the lead by setting the table and adding her own special flair and decor. As she gets older, give her defined responsibilities around the house, something she has 100 percent responsibility over, like the care and feeding of pets, fixing breakfast on Sunday, or maintaining flower beds.

Challenge your Biathlete to be a hero and use his courage to stand up for what's right. Talk about biblical heroes who were dared to do right against all odds of success and survival. Tell the stories of Daniel's life.

Naps are perfect for Biathlete kids who go, go, go but can get demanding and contrary if they don't have enough rest. With your preschooler Biathlete, try an active morning with a nap after lunch. If your Biathlete is in school, he might need a short catnap when he gets home.

Sometimes a Biathlete's competitive nature will manifest through arguing with you. Be willing to explain the "why" to her, but also reinforce that you are the parent, that she will always have authorities in her life, and that she will have to submit even when she doesn't want to. (Except when she knows she is being ordered to do something wrong.) Take time to understand each other, but remind her that *understanding doesn't equal agreement.*

Taking the time to listen to her means you understand her, not necessarily that you agree with her.

ARRHYTHMIA?

As you study these four heartprints, you may find that you are a mix of two or more. This is fairly common and perhaps even to be expected. Depending on the situation and what's expected of us, we may have the ability to switch from one heartprint to another. You have one dominant heartprint, which is how you *prefer* to pace yourself; this is the one that feels most natural and normal. Even so, you might switch to your secondary heartprint if the environment calls for it. For instance, if you're a Runner and find yourself in a hostile work situation, you may have to focus solely on getting the task done and not relating to everyone around you. You may have to be more in touch with your "inner Walker self," who takes things more slowly, more deliberately, and with fewer people.

Be sure to make allowances for all four heartprints in your family. Don't show preference to your son because he's a Runner like you. Don't isolate your daughter because she's a Cruiser who doesn't enjoy running full speed with you. Consider Dr. Phil McGraw's astute advice:

> No child stands above another, and as a parent, you should never play favorites. Children sense favoritism, and they often interpret it as a lack of love. It leaves a residue that can show up later as low self-esteem.
>
> So the message should be obvious: A spirit of acceptance is a core requirement for nurturing and building a phenomenal family. When you exhibit a spirit that says you accept your children, you're saying that even though you may not always rubber-stamp things your kids are doing, you love them. You're saying that despite all the things you sometimes

wish they would do or wouldn't do, the bottom line is that you accept who they are, and you will always be there for them. *When children live with acceptance, approval and praise, they learn to like themselves, they learn to have faith in themselves and they learn to love.*[5]

DISCUSSION QUESTIONS

Parent to Parent

1. What do you like to do on weekends? Do you cocoon? If so, how does this play out for you?
2. Have you seen evidence in your life of "leisure sickness"?
3. Which of the following have you used?
   a. "Everyone is living this way."
   b. "I don't have any other choice."
   c. "Successful people are always busy."
   d. "I have to do this to pay for my lifestyle."
   e. "It's going to slow down soon—this is just a phase."
4. Are you or any of your family members a Biathlete? What characteristics stand out?
5. What are some subtle ways we show explicit or implicit favoritism or prejudice to our kids in ways we may not even notice?

Parent and Child

1. Ask, "What do you think we should do on weekends?"
2. Review the characteristics of a Biathlete (in chapter 6 and above) with your child. Ask, "Do these fit you and/or another family member?"
3. Ask, "When do you feel my approval and acceptance the most?"

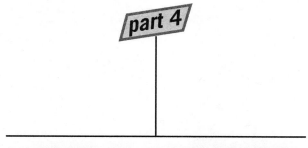

part 4

MAKING YOUR HEARTPRINT
WORK FOR YOUR FAMILY

CHAPTER ELEVEN

Making Time

I've met some very successful people. Many of these are wealthy, articulate, educated, cultured, and respected—*except by their kids.* What is it that's caused these men and women to excel at work and fail at home?

Recently, one such couple was in my family coaching office, tears filling the eyes of both. Hurting, the husband asked, "How can we be successful at work and having a breakdown at home?"

"Parenting is succeeding in a different way," I explained.

Their foreheads wrinkled. "Whaaat?" the wife wondered.

"The skills, talents, and lifestyle that spell success in business and the professions can actually work against you in your role as a parent. Both moms and dads are urged to develop their skills for the marketplace, sometimes even at the neglect of developing tools or skills for being married or being a parent. Most 'Runner parents' are rattled when they discover that child-rearing, for them, can be more challenging and annoying than being a success in their job. While it may not in fact be more difficult, you do need a different set of tools—you need to develop life skills to help you parent."

"People respect me at work," he explained, wiping his eyes. "They treat me with kindness and deference. When I get home, my kids are disrespectful and mean—to me and to each other. I don't get it."

"The truth is that what works at the office isn't always

effective at home. In fact, super-achievers often are mediocre parents: Their single-minded focus on work keeps them from time-consuming relationships with their spouse and children. Runners tend to be highly competitive and can view people—even people within their own family—as tools, steppingstones, or obstacles. Does that make sense?"

"I do that," she confessed. "I usually see the kids as an interruption to what I really want to accomplish. Hurdles I have to jump over en route to the finishing line—getting the task done or seeing the deal closed."

"And I'm competitive—just ask my wife." (She smiled and nodded vigorously.) "I hate to lose, and I'm impatient. We didn't have our kids until we were both thirty; I think we still liked the idea of going fast and furious, like we did before. Now it's slow and infuriating."

"Let me ask you a question that all midlife parents need to ask: Where do you want success—at home or at work?"

"Does it have to be one or the other?" she asked.

"Yeah, can it only be one? If we fail at work, we won't have the lifestyle we want to give our kids; we won't be able to send them to college. And if we succeed with business while our kids get messed up, what good is that? Can't it be both?"

"Yes, it *can* be both. You can be an effective parent *and* a successful worker. But here's the key: You must develop a set of skills on the home front that are as developed and effective as your work skills."

"Sounds good." He grabbed his wife's hand. "Where do we start?"

"You—*each* of you—becomes 'the relaxed parent.' You learn to help them do more as you do less."

"Sounds *glorious!*" she exclaimed, waving her arm through a sweeping arc.

"The relaxed parent doesn't allow his or her worth to be determined by vocation. She does not allow how others treat her to affect how she feels or what she believes about herself. He does not allow the ups and downs of the market, the cash flow, or the press releases to determine his worth as a man.

"The relaxed parent is self-confident but not afraid to learn or to ask for help. The relaxed parent does not look at her kids as symbols but as persons. The relaxed parent takes the time to study them, to know them, to see how they're like her and different from her. When you're rushed, you don't take the time to see children as multifaceted human beings; instead you stereotype them as 'my son the skateboarder' or 'my daughter the Irish dancer,' missing what's beyond the externals. *Missing out on connecting.*"

"That's us, exactly," he acknowledged.

"And when we treat kids as symbols, they tend to act out."

"Do you have a video camera on our house?" she teased. "You nailed it. That's exactly how we live."

"I'm thrilled that all of this is resonating with you. However, don't see yourself as failures—try seeing yourselves as needing to take a course on new technology. Parenting is like software in that you have to update frequently for it to work. Even though you haven't kept up, you can catch up. Read and discuss this chart, and we'll go over it next week. It's something I adapted from a book I read years ago."[1] I handed them the following:

Qualities Needed to Succeed

At Work	*At Home*
1. Constant striving for perfection	Allowance for repeated errors
2. Mobility	Stability

3. Freedom from time constraints to pursue an independent life	Plenty of time for family activities
4. Impatience	Patience
5. Goal-oriented attitude toward the project at hand	Emphasis on process, surprises, and change as the child matures
6. Total commitment to yourself	Total commitment to others
7. Stubborn self-will	Softness, willingness to bend
8. Efficiency	Tolerance for chaos
9. Belief that success must always be top priority	Understanding that failure promotes growth
10. Controlling nature that enjoys directing others	Desire to promote independence in others even if their ways are not your ways
11. Concern for image	Relaxed acceptance of embarrassment
12. Firmness	Gentleness
13. Sense that nobody is as smart as you	True respect for your child's activities, free from comparison with your own
14. Preference for concise information	Ability to listen patiently while children talk
15. Exploitation of others	Ability to put child's needs first

Just look at these contrasts. Your children don't respond to you like people at work because they're not your employees or colleagues. They're your children. When you leave work and cross the border to your home, imagine that you're going to a different country. It *is,* in fact, another culture.

FAMILY TIME

Balancing the demands of work and the requirements of family isn't easy—it requires discipline, patience, planning, and diplomacy. Most of us more naturally tilt our time toward work—at least there we can see short-term results from our efforts.

Let's be honest: Family time doesn't always go so well. Little kids bring the challenges of fussing, spilling, and pouting. Teenagers might huff and roll their eyes at the very concept, and if you do manage to wrestle them into cooperation, you're likely to get such painful silence or volatile protest that you long for the days of fussing, spilling, and pouting.

I have startling news: *It's not supposed to be easy.* Family life is difficult!

Tim Stafford says it this way:

> Family togetherness isn't *supposed* to be a constant joy. You're setting a foundation to build lives on. Foundations aren't made of glamorous materials, but they hold houses together. Day in, day out, mealtimes bring us together. Warm memories come later.[2]

Building a solid and healthy family takes work. Laying the foundation with rudimentary stuff isn't enchanting, but it's necessary. In residential construction, the foundation is time-consuming; by comparison, *framing* the house goes quickly. We may have to labor for years on our family's foundation before we see results.

Families provide the raw materials for spiritual growth. In a family we learn about kindness, forgiveness, and reconciliation. The family environment provides for the teaching of spiritual truth—families are labs that instruct us on love and life. Families are where we can be ourselves—the best and the worst of each of us.

> All you who fear GOD, how blessed you are!
> How happily you walk on his smooth straight road!
> You worked hard and deserve all you've got coming.
> Enjoy the blessing! Revel in the goodness!
> Your wife will bear children as a vine bears grapes,
> your household lush as a vineyard,
> The children around your table
> as fresh and promising as young olive shoots.
> Stand in awe of God's Yes.
> Oh, how he blesses the one who fears GOD! (Psalm 128 THE MESSAGE)

God blesses us with variety; each child is different. Like a vineyard that produces different kinds of grapes, our families are evidence of God's grace and promise. We need to appreciate the beautiful and unique ways the Designer has designed each of us, beginning with our children.

One way of affirming His handiwork is to note how the heartprints complement one another (illustrated by the following diagram).

Heartprint Quadrant

High Activity

WALKER *Steady* Likes routine Loyal Patient Thoughtful Avoids conflict Consistent	RUNNER *Fast* Likes people Involved Intuitive Influential Takes risks Creative
CRUISER *Slow* Likes details Organized Industrious Analytical Makes lists Compliant	BIATHLETE *Fast and stop, fast and stop* Likes variety Strategic Bold Leads Curious Competitive

Low Activity   *Slow* <   Speed of Activity   > *Fast*

Heartprint Echocardiograms

Cruiser: Low level of activity; slow pace (low frequency)

Walker: Mid to high level of activity; slow to medium pace (low to medium frequency)

Runner: High level of activity; fast pace (high frequency)

Biathlete: Lower level of activity than Runner; pace alternates between very fast and very slow (various frequencies)

CONTINUING TO DISCOVER YOUR HEARTPRINT

The Heartprint Quadrant shows how Walkers and Runners love lots of activity; Walkers prefer a steady pace, while Runners like to move it along. Cruisers prefer fewer activities at a slow pace. Biathletes want to mix it up: rapids followed by restfulness, speedily moving along until they hit the wall, then desiring to do nothing until they recharge.

The echocardiograms can further help you to conceptualize the various heartprints. One way of determining yours is to think about what tends to frustrate you.

If you're a Cruiser, the frantic Runner who frenetically spins through a room is likely annoying. The painstaking, deliberate Cruiser is a probable irritation for the Runner. Walkers are often irked by the seeming inconsistency (stop and go) of Biathletes. The Biathlete might be aggravated by the Walker's pedantic, measured routine, perhaps sensing a lack of strategy and ambition.

Because our requests reveal our inner needs and often disclose our preferences for the speed(s) at which we live our lives, another way of honing in on your heartprint is to ask, *What do I request?*

If you find yourself requesting fewer activities, especially if you want to do one or two things at a relaxed, unhurried pace, you may be a Cruiser. If, for instance, you seek opportunities to do two or three faster-paced things for a while and then take time away, you might be a Biathlete. If you ask for scenarios that include moderate activity level at a medium pace—"Not too fast, not too slow, not too much"—you could be a Walker. And if your default request is "Give me *lots* of things to do and bring them on *now,*" you're likely a Runner.

A third significant way to further discern your heartprint is to ask, *If everything else is equal—if it were simply a matter of my choice—then which heartprint is most appealing to me? Which seems like the best fit? Which would I most often choose to live in (and live out)?*

Knowing your heartprint will help you as you seek time for your family to be together. You'll know what works best for you, and you'll discover how to design family time that acknowledges and affirms the uniquenesses of all the various heartprints represented in your family.

SETTING CARVED-OUT TIME TO BE TOGETHER

I am very interested in saving childhood—our culture is filled with people rushing through it and permitting erosion of the boundaries that protect it. I wish more of the effort that goes toward saving animals would go toward our kids, because childhood is an endangered species.

Some alert communities have noticed this dire condition and have decided to put their foot down. When an entire community stomps, it's with a big foot! *Harried citizens, take a night off.*

No homework, no practice, no clarinet lessons. No math league, no soccer, no SAT sessions. No swim meet, no Scout meet, no learning to sing. None of their usual scheduled things! Not tonight anyway, not in this town known for affluent, competitive, accomplished parents and children.

It took a committee of eighteen people seven months and six meetings to plan it, but Ridgewood—where the calculus tutorial runs into the orthodontist appointment, followed immediately by the strength-training class—is finally taking what heretofore only a blizzard could impose: a night off.

The night had its genesis last year, when harried mother of three, Marcia Marra, realized how overscheduled her family was. She formed a committee to discuss the problem, and it talked about programs and discussion groups.

We said, "Wait, we're working against ourselves," says the

Rev. Douglas Fromm. "Let's plan a night where nothing is planned." The idea caught on, particularly after September 11 [of 2001], when [this] New Jersey village of 30,000 lost twelve residents. From a hill, you could see the World Trade Center fall. "People began to think about what's really important," Fromm says.

School officials promised a homework amnesty. Sports teams canceled games and practices. Churches called off evening classes.

Family Night's success will be measured only by each participant. Marra says, "We don't even want quality time; we just want more downtime."

This being Ridgewood, someone asked for a list of suggested activities, but that was rejected as too well planned. And everyone laughed when someone else asked whether there'd be a prize for the family that had the best night off together.[3]

I like the thought of Marcia Marra: "We don't even want quality time; we just want more downtime."

I can relate. Can you?

Our community developed a similar program: *40 Days for the Family*, with a tagline of "It's about time." We encouraged families to spend time together learning, laughing, and building memories. We partnered with churches, businesses, nonprofits, and schools to highlight and affirm the theme of family. Response was phenomenal, with tens of thousands participating each year. It was my impression that we gave families permission to take time to be together. Some didn't yet know how to do it, so we offered ideas and produced activities. (For more information check out *www.40days.org*.)

Tim Stafford understands the challenges of making time for one another in today's family:

The modern world is not family-friendly. Its conscious-
ness is built on the individual—individual tastes, rights,
opinions and careers. Family comes in second place. Therefore families don't hold together in love. Since our culture
does not support family very deeply, family culture must do
so.[4]

24/7 @ ORD

Waiting at Gate C-6 in Chicago's O'Hare Airport, I picked
up the front page of a *USA Today,* and one article caught my eye
with its first sentence: "*Twenty-four-seven* isn't just an expression;
it's a cultural earthquake that's changing the way we live." I'd just
presented a parenting seminar in a nearby suburb, it was now
11:20 P.M., and I was soon flying back to Los Angeles. I'd arrive
about two, drive home, get to bed around three, be up by seven,
and speak to a large group at nine.

Twenty-four-seven . . . no kidding!

Thank heaven for 7-Eleven, the store that stays open day and
night. This week I went there to buy a gallon of milk—at five in
the morning. Now, some grocery stores have joined the ranks. You
can live 24/7 with ATMs; send e-mail till the wee hours; browse
your favorite store (in your bathrobe) at midnight; text message
your teens at 1:30 A.M. Sometimes only the pesky requirement of
sleep keeps us from being busy all twenty-four hours.

One of the reasons most of us haven't taken time to consider
our heartprint is that we're too scheduled. It wasn't too long ago
that our culture recognized and affirmed the need for a change of
pace. Sundays were protected from unnecessary activity. Most
stores were closed; few people worked; no kids' sports were scheduled; and the day was seen as special—the Lord's Day or Sabbath.
Now, in the era of 24/7, all the days blur into one. No day is set
apart. Each day is seen as the same.

With Sundays set aside, apart from all else, we at least had an afternoon to nap, chat, or connect with family or friends. On that special day we could appreciate a sense of closure to one week, resting so as to anticipate with freshness the beginning of the next. Sundays acted like a period in a sentence.

A time to pause.

A time to break.

A time to breathe.

To keep all our days from blurring together, we must build boundaries that hold back the unfinished backlog of life on one side and the countless enticing opportunities from technology, success, and wealth on the other.

RESTORING THE FAMILY SABBATH

Nothing in popular culture supports the notion of the Sabbath. Leisure is big, but the classic concept of breaking routine for renewal, worship, and reconnection is in disrepute. Let me suggest three ways to resurrect the Sabbath with your family.

The first idea is to *have a family huddle on Sunday afternoons or evenings.* The point isn't what you do as much as "we will be together." Protect the time. Don't allow sports, work, or hobbies to intrude. If Sunday doesn't work, choose another day; the essential thing is making time for each other, no matter how much time that is.

A family huddle could be a time to talk, laugh, take a walk, have ice cream. It doesn't have to be a teaching time or a serious discussion. Keep it casual, make it fun, but be consistent. Some families start with a snack, place the family calendar in front of them, and talk about what each member has coming up that week. This helps to coordinate activities, lend support, include everyone, *and* affirm the Cruiser and Walker who may not have as many events as the Runner or Biathlete.

The second idea to support the Sabbath is to *have a meal together.* Many families have discovered that a barbeque on Sunday evening works well during spring and summer. Remember that earlier we discussed the findings that a regular family meal helps our kids be better students and better people. Overall, begin eating together at least once or twice a week with your kids—you don't even have to cook it! All the research studies report that the important element is the dialogue around the table, not the quality or source of food.

Why is this important? Why have Columbia University, the National Honor Society, the National Institutes of Health, and other institutions found a link between a family dinner and better academic performance and health in children? Because *everyone is important at the table.* We share the meal and we share life. Eating together meets our most basic needs: nutrition, security, belonging, engagement, support, challenge, and fun. When we help prepare the food (even if it's only taking it out of the McDonald's bags), we're learning teamwork; when we stop what we're doing and sit down together, we're learning community; when we bow our heads and thank God for His provision, we're affirming our faith; when we pass the food and show good manners, we're demonstrating kindness and civility; when we each talk about our day, we're feeling connected and not isolated; when we share opinions or even disagreements, we're affirming individuality.

(And you thought you were just eating fast food!)

Psychological research demonstrates that when our kids (particularly teenagers) engage in lively discussion by sharing their opinions, they're using a part of their brain that's rapidly developing. This explains why they like to argue so much—it's a new muscle they're trying to exercise! This is also why kids who have a family dinner several times a week will do better at school—their brains are more engaged.

The National Honor Society has found that the only common link between their student members is regular family dinners together. The common denominator isn't parents' education or intelligence, attendance at an advantaged school, socioeconomic status, ethnicity, or any other factor. Amazingly, the one common denominator is that high achievers have family dinners!

If you cancel the tutor, stop the enrichment classes, throw away the SAT prep CD course, pull the plug on the TV, and sit down to a family dinner, it just might raise your kid's GPA. Say to him or her, "I have a plan to help you get better grades, and it doesn't involve homework or my nagging—interested?"

The third idea for restoring the family Sabbath is to *design a formalized break from routine.* This is controlling the elements of our life that usually control us, liberating ourselves from the diversions and demands of the week. Start by protecting a two- to four-hour period. During that time, do no work. Relax. Reconnect with your family and with God.

Attend church together as a family, have a meal together, play a table game or take a walk, then take naps! Start with these basics and adjust as you go. (I like to suggest Sundays, but if, for example, you attend church on Saturday evenings or another time, adapt your protected time as best fits your family.)

SEVEN POINTERS FOR MAKING TIME FOR YOUR FAMILY

1. Develop and maintain a consistent routine and pace of family life.
2. Make sure your family's collective heartprint includes and affirms the heartprint of each family member.
3. Maintain family as a top priority with your money and your time.
4. Teach and model family values (honesty, compassion, responsibility, etc.).

5. Create and maintain unique family traditions to strengthen belonging and reinforce your family's identity.
6. Establish clear expectations for behavior that are rooted in values and reinforced with consequences.
7. Require loyalty and personal accountability from each family member.

RITES OF PASSAGE

One of the creative ways to affirm the heartprint of each child is to develop, for and with them, meaningful rites of passage. We live in a culture that has erased the markers between little kids, kids, young teens, older teens, and adults—it's all equal-access now. Our children are exposed to adult concerns, issues, and entertainment without the skills or experience to process them. You can help to rebuild needed markers by establishing rites of passage for your children as they mature.

The following are some of the key events you might want to recognize:

- Potty training
- Getting dressed by themselves
- First day of kindergarten
- First day of first grade
- Accepting Christ
- First Communion
- Baptism
- Elementary graduation
- First day of middle school
- Welcome to puberty!
- Blessing ceremony
- Sweet! I'm sixteen!
- High school graduation

Those are just thirteen occasions to affirm your child and celebrate his or her progressive maturation toward adulthood. A rite of passage is a ritual that commemorates your child's growth in a way that's meaningful to her and reflective of your family's values. A rite of passage makes accommodations for each heartprint, seeking to affirm and include each member but highlighting the heartprint of the one who is the focus. In other words, an effective rite of passage moves along fast enough for the Runner and Biathlete but not so fast that it loses the Cruiser and Walker. Accordingly, it will have a mix of paces.

A few guidelines to consider:

1. With your child in mind, review the chapters on the four heartprints. Plan a rite of passage that reflects her heartprint.

2. If your child is over ten, involve him in the planning of the rite. He doesn't have to know everything (some elements can be kept for a surprise).

3. Root your rite in a biblical passage and develop a key principle that you hope to reinforce through the ceremony. For instance, the first day of middle school might be the perfect time to talk about courage and strength in a land of adversaries. Consider talking about Joshua (1:6–9).

4. Illustrate the *letting go/picking up* principle. You, the parent, are letting go of something, and she, the child, is picking up the responsibility and privilege of something new. This affirms the principle of *helping your child do more as you do less.*

5. Make it fun! Rites of passage are intended to affirm and celebrate, not scold or teach; they are an acknowledgment and affirmation of growth that has already occurred. In contrast to birthday parties that focus on gifts, a rite of passage focuses on growth: "He's reached this milestone!"[5]

DISCUSSION QUESTIONS

Parent to Parent

1. Review the chart *Qualities Needed to Succeed* and discuss: How is parenting "succeeding in a different way"?
2. Are you different at work than at home? In what ways?
3. Discuss this bumper sticker slogan: "No success can compensate for failure at home."
4. What are some ways we can affirm our child whose heartprint is different from ours?
5. Describe some ways God can use all heartprints in a family to facilitate individual growth and collective balance.

Parent and Child

1. Discuss the Heartprint Quadrant with your child; ask what qualities best describe her or him (and in what ways).
2. Ask your child to describe a time when he or she felt included in your family, felt comfortable with the family's pace.
3. Ask, "What are some family manners and traditions we have that show people to be more important than tasks?" (Example: "We don't bring homework to the dinner table.")

CHAPTER TWELVE

Malibu Marsha

A gleaming black limousine sped up the Pacific Coast Highway, one mile northwest of Malibu. The turbulence caused by its velocity almost blew the hiker out of the bike lane and into the brush.

"Always in a hurry," he muttered to himself, pausing to take in the morning sun warming the azure waters and the gaggle of surfers. He reached back to his pack for his water bottle. *Almost empty.* Glancing around and seeing a nearby beach house, he ran his hand through his jet-black hair. *Going to be a scorcher today.* A thin dirt road, almost completely hidden by overgrowth, led toward the beach; he pushed his sunglasses up the bridge of his nose and headed down.

The sandy path wove through the low-lying coastal brush and dumped into the little beachside cottage overlooking the surf. He took his last sip from the water bottle. *Perhaps they'll have something to drink.* He ambled past an ancient van with a crudely stenciled peace sign in the front where "VW" typically went. Though the lime-green paint had faded with its years, he could tell that at one time it was psychedelic.

A friendly, dusty black Lab hobbled over, mouth rimmed with white and gray hair.

"Hey, old boy. What's your name?" He bent over and petted the dog, scratching behind his ears.

"His name is Lazarus!" shouted a young woman standing in

the doorway, cradling a large blue pot and propping open the wood-framed screen with her foot. "Can I help you?" She looked beyond him to spot his car, or to determine if he was alone.

He looked up from the dog and brushed his hands together to wipe off any ticks, fleas, or germs. "Sorry to barge in on you, but could I bother you for some water?"

She carried the heavy pot to a crude wooden table on the porch and set it down with a plop. "You don't have a car?"

"No ma'am, I'm on foot. Enjoying the beautiful Malibu morning." He wiped at the sweat on his brow.

She chuckled in amusement.

"Something wrong?" He motioned toward her.

"Nah. You got somethin' on your . . ." She pointed to her right temple.

"What?"

"Some dirt on your head. Sorry, probably got it off Lazarus. He gets dirty running around the bluffs and the beach."

Running? More like limping. He grinned as he watched Lazarus "chase" after a rabbit.

"Wanna wash up? I'll get you that water."

"That would be good. But I don't want to impose."

"Nonsense! Use the utility sink around the porch and I'll grab a fresh towel and my water jug. How about some lemonade?"

"Perfect, thank you." He stepped up on the bare wooden porch that appeared to have been built out of used shipping pallets. Finding the plastic sink, he scrubbed his hands and face.

"Here you are." She thrust a mint green towel at him.

"Thanks." The cool water was refreshing. He ran his sunglasses under the tap and wiped them with the hand towel.

"Gotta have a clean windshield," she said with a wry smile. She wore a sleeveless denim shirt and white cargo shorts. Toned and tanned. Light brown hair sun-streaked with blond highlights.

No makeup or jewelry. Her smile revealed straight teeth and suggested orthodontist visits as a teen, which, by his guess, was about twenty years ago.

"Really appreciate this." He took the proffered glass with his right hand, then switched it to his left and stuck out his right to shake hers. "Hi, I'm Chad."

She brushed the cold dampness from her hand. "Nice to meet ya. I'm Marsha Bethany. Here, have a seat, Chad. I'll go get that lemonade."

"Great." He plopped into a white wooden Adirondack chair. "Cooking something?"

"Yeah, some crabs," she replied over her shoulder.

"Can I help?" He leaned forward as much as he could.

"Oh, don't be silly. I'll take care of it. Wait here—I'll be right back." Marsha lifted a single-burner Coleman stove from underneath the table, fired it up, and set the big pot on top. She smiled at him and then disappeared into the cottage.

Chad sighed, opened the top two buttons on his shirt, and eased back in the chair. He closed his eyes and soaked up the sunshine.

"Here you are." Marsha had a pitcher of lemonade and a platter of crackers, cheese, grapes, and dates. "Thought you might be hungry."

"Actually, I am. Looks wonderful." He reached for a Wheat Thin and Colby cheese.

"Make yourself at home—I have to finish a few things inside. Be right back."

He munched, then reclined and was quickly asleep.

"Excuse me. Um, excuse me?"

Chad lifted his glasses and rubbed his eyes. "Huh?"

"Are you Marsha's friend? I didn't know she was expecting anyone."

His eyes focused on a young brunette standing before him, backlit by the cascading sun. "Sorry. I must have dozed off. Chad Rivers." He took off his shades, leaned forward, and stuck out his hand.

She wore a pink tank top with white calf-length pedal pushers and had a slight glow from being at the beach. "Nice to meet you." With a timid smile, she slowly offered her hand. "What brings you to our humble abode?"

"Just passing through. I'm on foot, heading north. Only stopped in for water, but Marsha is taking good care of me. And you are?"

"Maureen. Marsha's *much* younger sister," she toyed.

"She's very hospitable."

"That she is. Lots of energy. Works from sunup to sundown. She built this deck herself, and she turned this old dump into a shabby chic beach cottage. Oh, and she's making dinner."

"So I hear." He sipped his lemonade. "What do you do, Maureen?"

"I'm a student. At Pepperdine." She twirled her mahogany-colored hair around her index finger.

"What's your major?"

"Psychology, with a minor in religion."

"Like it?"

"*Love* it, and it's just down the street."

"What a location. The view is unmatched—beautiful."

"Yeah, it is. I always enjoy being close to the ocean."

"Maureen!" Marsha peeked around the porch. "Did you meet Chad?"

"Just getting acquainted, yes."

"Did you bring the herbs from the beach?"

"On the kitchen counter."

"Thanks." Marsha headed inside.

"Now, where were we? Oh yeah, tell me about yourself: Why don't you have a car? What's up north?" Maureen sat down, cross-legged. "Fill me in!"

As he answered all of her questions, she asked more. Finally, she spoke in declaration. "I'm sorry for all my queries. I'm just a hugely inquisitive person—I like to learn from everyone I meet. People hurry around, scurrying by each other, missing out on life's little big things." She glanced at Marsha, now hanging laundry on the clothesline. She shifted her weight on the deck.

"How rude of me—please sit in the chair." Chad leaned forward to get up.

"No, thank you, I actually prefer the floor. That's why there's only one chair out here."

"Do you live here with your sister?"

"Yes, my sister, Miss Busy Bee. She never relaxes."

"She's welcoming," he laughed as he held up the cheese platter.

"Absolutely, she is, but she's constantly distracted by *tasks tasks tasks,* and she gets upset because I don't always help her. Her favorite line is, 'Why do I have to do all of the work around here?' I tell her no one is making her and ask her to rest awhile, but she won't. I don't think she can."

"She handles the details, you focus on the people."

"Exactly."

"Maureen! Can you start on the salad?" Marsha shouted from the kitchen window.

"Marsha! Marsha! Marsha! Why does it always have to be 'Can you this?' 'Can you that?' Can't you just chill a little?" Maureen huffed, turned back, and quietly said, "See what I mean?"

"Maureen, Marsha is stressed about many things, but only

one thing is needed. You have chosen wisely, and what you have chosen will not be taken away from you."

She blushed. "Thanks, Chad. Those are such kind words." She tilted her head. "By the way, do you see many sci-fi movies?" As she shifted her leg she accidentally knocked over her lemonade, spilling it all over his feet. "Oh! Let me clean that up." She yanked a beach towel from the railing, pulled off his leather slip-ons, and dabbed at the sticky liquid on his toes. As she leaned, her hair fell forward onto the top of his feet.

"Hey, I saw *this* in a movie once," he quipped. "Are you anointing me?"

"Yeah, right!"

DOERS AND RELATERS

Don't fret: this is still a book on fast families. I just wanted to retell a story I paraphrased from the New Testament about the sisters Martha and Mary.[1]

Martha, aka Marsha, is a doer. Her name means "lady," and in the scriptural account she was the lady of the house, concerned with operating it smoothly, efficiently, and impressively. She was given to hospitality, a kind of Martha Stewart of the day (but without the jail time, so far as we know). She had lots of energy, and she used it to make sure everything was perfect.

"But Martha was distracted by all the preparations that had to be made" (Luke 10:40). She was task-oriented, anxious to get the job done and agitated at any delay. She came to Jesus and asked, "Lord, don't you care that my sister has left me to do the work by myself? Tell her to help me!"

You can hear and even feel her stress and frustration. She hadn't accepted the different personality and pace of her sister—to Martha, Mary was irresponsible and lazy. Later in her life, we see Martha's grasp of spiritual knowledge and faith in her affirmation of belief that Jesus could bring back her brother, Lazarus, from the grave.[2] At *this* point in her growth, however, it's all about completing the project. She hasn't yet learned to embrace relationships and conversations for what they are—precious gems we hold in our palm for a few fleeting moments.

LEARNING FROM MARY

Mary wasn't as industrious—she was naturally more relational. She wasn't obsessed with the condition of the house or the preparations for dinner. She didn't keep a mental list of tasks, and she wasn't as proficient with busywork. Mary seized the opportunity to sit at the feet of an extraordinary friend.

Jesus affirmed Mary's judgment and rebuked Martha:

> "Martha, Martha," the Lord answered, "you are worried and upset about many things, but only one thing is needed. Mary has chosen what is better, and it will not be taken away from her" (Luke 10:41).

Isn't it encouraging that Jesus cares more about us than our performance? He doesn't say, "Get it all done, make it perfect, then I'll make an appearance." He says, "I want to be with you. Let's be together to relax and connect. The tasks can wait."

What can we learn from Mary?

We learn that it's the right call to sit at the feet of Jesus; when we do, we show our humility. We don't need the perfect table setting or a manicured lawn—it's not about our work anyway. It's about being followers of Christ. It's about our relationship, not our showcase of talent.

We discover that being quiet allows for spiritual reception; strident spiritual activity isn't as conducive. *We don't always have to be going to be growing.*

We see that when we sit at the feet of Jesus, we listen and learn.

We notice Mary at the feet of Jesus three times:

- Once for *connection* as she listened.[3]
- Once for *comfort* at the death of her brother.[4]
- Once for *service* as she anointed His feet with perfume and wiped them with her hair.[5]

Sitting involves sacrificing our busy schedule. Sitting means abandoning our lists. When we put our agendas aside and focus on being with Jesus, our world changes. Instead of it being all about us, it becomes all about Him. Do this and hear Him say,

> *Only one thing is needed, only one. You have chosen what is better, and it will not be taken away from you. Everything else can be taken away, or breaks, or is lost, or rusts; our friendship, our intimacy, cannot be taken away.*

When we embrace this closeness in our lives and in our families, a refreshing aroma fills our homes, just as when Mary poured expensive perfume over Jesus' feet: "And the house was filled with the fragrance of the perfume."[6]

Extravagant.

Scandalous.

Provocative.

Honorable.

THE PURPOSE OF YOUR HEARTPRINT

As you read the story about Marsha and Maureen, you may have noticed tendencies that reflect your family members. Your husband may be a relational Maureen, while you're the Marsha variety. You might be anxious about the flowers, the place mats, the pot roast, and the kids' behavior, while he's sitting in the living room chatting it up with your guests, without a concern to all the production involved for such a performance. *Doesn't he get it? Why can't he be more helpful, or at least considerate?*

In this case, the key is to realize that your husband isn't a mistake—he may *make* mistakes, but he isn't one. And neither are you—things *do* need to get done, in their appropriate time. Each family has a Marsha and a Maureen. Each family has members with a natural, God-given tendency to lean toward being a Mary (Maureen) or being a Martha (Marsha). God has placed within your family the people you need to grow and learn from . . . including the most challenging member!

If our family were all Cruisers, we'd get things done, because we'd all have lists to check off, but we wouldn't have much time for each other. If we were all Runners, we'd do lots of things together but come home to a mess. If we were all Walkers, we'd enjoy a steady routine that could easily slip into boredom. If we were all Biathletes, we'd be attacking each other because our various paces would often be off kilter ("Is it time to race or take a nap?").

Isn't God gracious *not* to give you a family of heartprints just like yours?

DISCUSSION QUESTIONS

Parent to Parent

1. Do you see yourself more like a Mary (Maureen) or a Martha (Marsha)? Do you give the same answer when you ask yourself the same question in relationship to (in the context of) the rest of your family?

2. Review some of the lessons we can learn from Mary (above). Which would you like to see become a more reg-

ular practice in your life? What are some basic steps toward implementing it?

3. Describe ways that God can use all four heartprints in a family to help all its members to grow individually and balance collectively.

Parent and Child

1. From Luke 10:38–42, read the biblical story of Martha and Mary to your child and ask, "Who in our family is Martha? Who is Mary? Why?"

2. Ask, "How does it make you feel when an adult sits on the ground or squats or sits to talk with you at your eye level?"

3. Ask, "What are more ways that we as a family can show that projects aren't as important as people?"

CHAPTER THIRTEEN

Kingdom Kids

One of the greatest scenes in the movie *Napoleon Dynamite* is when Napoleon's brother, Kip, finally gets married and sings an off-key tribute to his bride, LaFawnduh. He croons about his love for her with poetry he penned himself:

Why do you love me?
Why do you need me?
Always and forever. . . .
Yes, I love technology,
but not as much as you, you see.
But I still love technology
Always and forever.
Always and forever.[1]

It's hilarious.

Just like Kip, many of us have an enduring love for technology, *always and forever*.

Last December, I received one of those handy PDAs as a gift. The day after, I spent a big chunk of time entering data and playing with all the bells and whistles while my wife and daughters hit the mall for the melee otherwise known as "after-Christmas sales." I thought it was time well spent, and I appreciate the gift.

But a year later, I rummaged around for the warranty because I still felt hurried and disconnected. I was hoping that the small print guaranteed, "This powerful handheld computer will revolutionize your life, assist you in saying no to trivial distractions, and help you focus on truly essential endeavors. (Extra memory required.)"

I found no such promise.

So much for *always and forever.*

Then it occurred to me: Technology isn't the answer any more than moving to a mountain peak is the real solution. Regardless, we cannot continue living in congested loneliness, trying to manage a swarm of disconnected relationships and duties. It's not only exhausting, it's toxic.

In the West, particularly North America, we have crowned the individual as king, trumpeting individual pursuits and rights above all else. This view can be traced in part to the teachings of French philosopher Jean-Jacques Rousseau (1712–1778) and before him to the French mathematician René Descartes (1596–1650), who advanced self-orientated philosophy with his popular phrase, "I think, therefore I am." At the core, this perspective teaches that my identity comes from my *self.*

While this may seem like a harmless slogan tossed around by thinkers in powdered wigs, it has become the anthem for Americans as we march forward to the beat of our own drum. Our obsession with self has led to our disregard for any extrinsic reality or Supreme Being; those things don't matter because "It's all about me."

When self is king, we don't ask, "How might I bring my life within the scope of scriptural standards?" or "How can I live in order to honor a holy God?" In the world view of self, all absolutes—God and His Word—are under the authority of "What it all means to me" or "How it relates to my life" or "How it helps me get what I want." Whitney Houston sings "the greatest love of all" is to love yourself.

Our culture has placed secular materialism on center stage, marginalizing God to the corners of public life, preferably to the quiet niches of private life. Success is now determined by the next acquisition. Our net worth isn't determined by our character, by divine declarations, or by Holy Writ; our worth, no longer who we are, is now determined by what we have. We live by the modern mantra: *I own, therefore I am.*

I submit that our hurried and hectic lifestyles are a result of going along with this societal tide. We have been swept along by individualism, materialism, and secularism . . . and most of us don't even know it.

It is our job as Christian parents to challenge the culture and raise our children with a different perspective—one that reflects principles of God's kingdom. It is our responsibility to raise countercultural children, not socialize them into the predominant culture. We are to be developing *kingdom kids*—kids with passion, conviction, and spiritual strength to advance God's kingdom.

A VIEW FROM ANOTHER CONTINENT

We can better understand our own culture, gaining a more objective perspective, by stepping outside of it and aiming to see it as others do. By and large, Africans have not been seized by a lifestyle of accumulation and individualistic thought; they take a more familiar and community-minded approach to life. I believe we can learn from them, and especially from the South African Anglican minister Desmond Tutu, who wrote, "A person can only be a person through others."[2]

Bishop Tutu seeks to promote *ubuntu,* which is an African term for "people," meaning an approach to life that upholds community theology and challenges Western ideals of individualism, materialism, and accumulation. His provocative teaching means our perceived personal value increases in direct proportion to our investment in community. In other words, our worth isn't determined by what we have but by what we give.

Tutu's teaching harmonizes with God's: "It is more blessed to give than to receive" (Acts 20:35). It also implies that we were created for community. Every human being was designed by the Creator with an innate need to connect with others.

When Adam was in the Garden, though creation was "all good," it wasn't enough: "It is not good for the man to be alone" (Genesis 2:18). God, in divine providence, knew that man could not deal with being alone, even in the ideal environment. Why didn't He create Eve at the same time? Randy Frazee explains:

> If God knew that man could not handle human isolation, why did he not deal with this up front on day six? I believe this is God's way of highlighting for us man's need for community. If God had created Eve on the sixth day, along with Adam, we might have taken for granted the absolute importance of companionship and conversation. I think God delayed the creation of Eve to drive the point home that humans have not been created to be alone. In other words, *community is the only change order in creation.* God is saying that he designed humans to require oxygen to live. By the same token, he is also saying that we must have community to live! We are built with a connection requirement.[3]

I like to speak to my parenting seminar audiences about how our culture has done an excellent job of affirming the individual. Our kids grow up with a strong sense of self; thanks to the messages they receive from toddler TV, they learn that each of them is "special." We have done a super job on teaching individuality—however, personal uniqueness and value is only half of the equation. We also need to teach our children community. *Individuality without a sense of community leads to narcissism.*

Are you concerned about the growing sense of entitlement lots of kids seem to have? Why many of them mope around with the what-have-you-done-for-me-lately mentality? We need to balance "you are special" messages with "you can contribute" messages. Imagine what could happen if each child realized he is a contributing and essential member of a team!

I attribute most of the malady of spoiled children to parents: They've gone along with the culture, affirming their child's individuality while failing to do equal work in helping their child develop connection with community. Frustrated parents call me in desperation and say, "I don't know how to fix my spoiled child!" This is usually a good place to start.

AMBER'S AMBUSH

It started out as a tranquil Christmas morning: coffee brewing, homemade sweet rolls in the oven, Rob and Cari waiting for the kids to wake up and start the festivities. This year it was going to be relaxing—no flights from crowded terminals, no long-distance drives on slick roads, no hassles . . . just the four of them huddled around the fireplace and the sparkling tree. Though it had been a financially prosperous year, Rob and Cari decided to buy only one present for each other and put most of their Christmas budget toward gifts for Matt and Amber and toward the family snowboarding vacation to Colorado they'd take in January.

Matt woke up first and stumbled down the stairs, the fragrant scent of his favorite treat drawing him into the kitchen. "Are they ready yet?"

"Five minutes. Merry Christmas, sleepyhead." Cari gave him a hug.

"C'mon, Mom," he brushed her off. "I can't wait, I'm starved."

"Wait till your sister gets up."

He padded out and stumbled up the stairs.

"*Go!* Get out of here, Matty!" Amber screamed a minute later from her bedroom.

"Get jumpin', Amb—we're all downstairs waiting. More beauty sleep isn't going to help you now!" He pulled on her foot, sticking out of the covers.

"Mom! Matt is *buggin'* me!"

Rob looked up from reading the paper by the fire. "So much for peace on earth, goodwill toward men."

Cari set her baked egg dish onto a trivet on the dining table. "It was nice while it lasted."

BAM.

"Mom!"

Matt flew down the stairs with Amber in chase, swinging her pillow in fury. "He pulled me out of bed. I'm gonna kill him!"

Cari finally corralled the situation by announcing breakfast. After getting through the meal without incident, they settled into soft seats by the fire. Rob read the Christmas story from Luke and then prayed, thanking God for the ultimate gift of His Son and the joy they shared as a family.

Within minutes, they commenced with presents. Matt and Amber dove into the mound of gifts, ripping paper and ribbons from the clothes, CDs, techno-gadgets, and gift cards for stores they'd hit the next day. Fifteen minutes later there was a three-foot-high pile of rubble.

Suddenly Amber was kicking through the debris with intense determination. "Where is it?"

"Where is what?" asked Cari.

"That outfit we looked at in the mall? You were there, Mom—Junior's Jungle? You know, the cute outfit I picked, the blue one? You were going to get it for me for Christmas—where is it?"

"Oh, I found the green one on sale at Macy's instead. It's right there." She pointed to the opened box.

"That's not what you said!"

"What?" Cari moved her head back in disbelief.

"You had me try it on, and you *said* you'd get it for me for Christmas."

"No, I didn't."

"Yes, you did!"

"I said *maybe* I'd get it for you for Christmas. That was five weeks ago."

"You *promised*."

"Amber, look at all the stuff you have." Rob gestured toward the mound of gifts at her feet. "You have no right to complain."

"You always take *her* side." Amber kicked the green-outfit box at the fireplace, rattling the screen.

"Ungrateful brat," Matt muttered under his breath.

"Forget *you*! I've had it with this family. Bunch of liars. You treat me like a baby. *I hate you!*" She spun around and stomped out.

Rob and Cari stared at each other with mouths agape, trying to figure out how Christmas morning had gone south.

Within a few moments, Amber reappeared in sweats with a backpack, storming out the front door and slamming it with a vengeance.

You'd be concerned if your daughter was going to run away. You'd perhaps be disappointed if she was upset that she didn't get the Christmas present she wanted, and regardless, you'd run after her if she was eight, or twelve, or fourteen. But what would you do if she was twenty?

Amber ambushed Christmas and threw a tantrum at *twenty*.

The next day Rob called me, earnestly asking, "Where did we go wrong? We tried to raise them by giving them the best, by giving them our support, our attention. Where did we blow it?" *Individuality without a sense of community leads to narcissism.*

IN THE WRINKLE OF TIME

Our entire Western world view has been shaped by individualism, even our perspective of time; like the Romans before us, we believe that "day" begins at sunrise and ends at sunset. Between sunrise and sunset were roughly twelve hours. Night, also twelve hours, was divided into four "watches": 6 to 9 P.M., 9 to midnight, midnight to 3, and 3 to 6 A.M., or sunrise the next day. Sundials were used in the palaces and homes of wealthy citizens, but the average person couldn't afford one, so they told time with phrases like "at the sixth hour."

Greek language and culture had given the term *chronos,* denoting a space or duration of time. *Chronos,* referring to specific and detailed time, is the root of words like "chronology" and "chronograph."

> Then Herod called the Magi secretly and found out from them the exact time *(chronos)* the star had appeared. (Matthew 2:7)

Before Greek and Roman influence, we find a much different time paradigm, especially within the more agrarian and nomadic Hebrew culture. The Hebrews began each day the evening before at 6 P.M. This practice was shaped by their view of God, who declared in Genesis 1:5 that "there was evening and there was morning—the first day."

So the Jewish day begins at dusk; the focus is on rest, refreshment, and reconnection. The ancient Hebrews would gather for a meal together around the fire, telling stories, enjoying song, narrating God's wonders to their children, and then nodding off for eight hours of sleep. After a twelve-hour day of labor, they didn't need to work out at the gym or take a sleeping pill. I like the way they organized their day: twelve hours for work, four hours for relationships, and eight hours for sleep.

What would happen if we did that?

The Hebrews followed God's rhythm. Their word for time, *'eth,* conceives of time as a series of recurring seasons, or as a particularly appropriate or opportune moment. This Eastern view sees time as *rhythm;* time has recurring cycles—days and weeks, months and seasons and years—and life itself follows the pattern of seasons.[4] While the Greek/Roman *chronos* view treats time as a series of segments or points, the Hebrews saw time as "in between." *In between* sunset and sunrise; *in between* sunrise and sunset; *in between* sunset and bedtime. *In between* God and people. *In between* parent and child. Hebrew theology left little room for individualism—it was all about connection and community.

We are privileged to see our role as parents from this perspective, as the *in between* connectors. Connecting spiritual truth with physical human beings (our children). Connecting abstract concepts with concrete illustrations. Connecting God's past faithfulness to trust for today and hope for the future. Connecting our hearts with theirs so they'll be assured of never being alone.

Our children cannot and will not be secure if all they have to count on is themselves. If we can help them connect with their roots, their ancestors, their family, and their distinctiveness as members of a faith community, we confer security, confidence, and purpose.

ESCAPING THE CURRENT

It takes effort to swim against the cultural current. It doesn't happen by accident. You have to be intentional. You have to know which way to go. And you have to be willing to fight the flow.

We need to get out of the current, swim to dry land, and climb to new heights for fresh perspective. When Jesus went up the mountain to deliver His sermon, of all the things He could have said, why did He focus on the few that would only take twenty-three minutes to deliver (the length of one episode of *The Simpsons*)? Consider these words:

> Be especially careful when you are trying to be good so that you don't make a performance out of it. It might be good theater, but the God who made you won't be applauding.
>
> When you do something for someone else, don't call attention to yourself. You've seen them in action, I'm sure— "playactors," I call them—treating prayer meeting and street corner alike as a stage, acting compassionate as long as someone is watching, playing to the crowds. They get applause, true, but that's all they get.
>
> When you help someone out, don't think about how it looks. Just do it—quietly and unobtrusively. That is the way your God, who conceived you in love, working behind the scenes, helps you out. (Matthew 6:1–4 THE MESSAGE)

Apart from answering why Christ addressed only a handful of matters at that particular time, we can see that His message is as appropriate for today as it was nearly two thousand years ago. In these verses, Jesus challenges us to deal with three issues that sweep us up in the cultural tide of hurriedness. I call them "The Three A's."

• Approval
• Achievement
• Acquisition

We overload our calendar because we hate to disappoint people. They may even be people we don't like! But because we're seeking their *approval,* we say yes, later resenting that we caved in.

We're driven by *achievement:* being first-chair violin, making the varsity team, graduating with honors, landing a promotion. There isn't anything inherently wrong with these notable accomplishments, but when they become the focus of our lives, with the goal of attracting attention to ourselves, they become taskmasters driving us to always be on top of the pile, regardless of what we have to do to get there.

Acquisition often results from constant pressure to have the latest fashion, car, vacation, technology, music, entertainment. Does Christ's admonition to "not let your left hand know what your right hand is doing" apply if the act or achievement or acquisition is something good? Don't we want others to know?

The answer is that we *do* need the approval and affirmation of another—but only one other.

We need the applause of One.

Incorporating this concept into our thoughts and actions liberates us from having to march for approval, to strive to achieve for accolades, to acquire so much stuff that we win. Jesus is calling us to get above the fray, and He offers us a lifesaver out of the cascading current, beckoning us to the summit.

> You're blessed when you're at the end of your rope. With less of you there is more of God and his rule. (Matthew 5:3 THE MESSAGE)

If we are to raise kingdom kids, we will need a kingdom perspective—one that advances the prominence of God, not ourselves.

In a way, growing kingdom kids is a spiritual discipline. It's not simple, it can't be done quickly, and it meets with all forms of resistance. It's easier to accommodate the crowd than to be disciplined. It's less hassle to float with the cultural tide than to swim out of it. Standing for what advances God's kingdom will bring rejection and ridicule.

All spiritual disciplines require a no factor and a go factor. There are things to avoid, and there are things to pursue. It's easier to watch TV than to read the Bible. It's easier to talk on the phone than to pray. It's easier to fill my life with activity and noise than to be still and reflect on God.

What's easier is not what we're called to do.

As people of faith who happen to be parents, we have a much higher calling. We are to be raising kingdom kids—children with passion, conviction, and influence to advance God's kingdom. The results of this noble pursuit not only endure forever but they also benefit people, especially our kids, infinitely more than approval, achievement, or acquisition.

Always and forever.

DISCUSSION QUESTIONS

Parent to Parent

1. What are some evidences of our love for technology? Do any of these strongly show up in our lives?
2. Dr. Benjamin Wiker says that "the self is the modern substitute for the soul."[5] What are some ways we see this in our culture? In our homes?
3. What are some ways in which we're caught up in the current of individualism, secularism, and materialism?
4. Knowing that our kids are watching us, what can we do to challenge individualism, secularism, and materialism? What can we do as a family?
5. What do you think about the concept of living for the applause of One?

Parent and Child

1. Discuss the value of team play. Discuss why it's important in team sports to play as a teammate rather than going for personal excellence.
2. If your kids are ten or older, watch *Napoleon Dynamite* and discuss how Napoleon, Pedro, and Deb challenge popular ideals and swim against the social tide of their high school.
3. Read aloud the true story of "Amber's Ambush" (above). Ask your child, "What went wrong?" Discuss ideas: "What could we do, in our family, to prevent this from happening?"

CHAPTER FOURTEEN

The Refreshing Family

Several years ago I was running on the treadmill of approval, achievement, and acquisition. As a youth and family pastor, I was responsible for middle school, high school, and, because our college pastor had resigned, college students and their families. On top of that, I was preaching on a regular basis and finishing a book. Now it was time for the fall retreat, and I had to plan it.

I was overwhelmed.

Soon, though, I came across a verse that changed my life and helped me slow down.

> At daybreak Jesus went out to a solitary place. The people were looking for him and when they came to where he was, they tried to keep him from leaving them. (Luke 4:42)

Ascertaining that Jesus modeled something I specifically needed to learn, I decided to begin learning it with my college students. I announced, "We're going to have a silent retreat—no speaker, no program, no distractions. It will be cheap, the accommodations will be sparse, the food will be good, and you'll be alone with God on Catalina Island for a weekend."

To my surprise, the camp filled up within days. A few weeks later, we loaded the boat and headed out to stay in rustic tent cabins, starting our retreat on Saturday after breakfast. For eight solitary hours we were to be silent, listening to God, reading the Bible, journaling, appreciating the splendor of creation. Sack lunches were provided, though many students opted to fast.

The solitude and the silence deeply impacted me. I hadn't been aware of how noisy and crowded my life had become. Meditating on the passage from Luke (as well as others), I related to how Jesus always seemed to be surrounded by people who wanted a piece of Him. I was encouraged to discover His pattern of withdrawing to rejuvenate after engagement.

> The news about him spread all the more, so that crowds of people came to hear him and to be healed of their sicknesses. But Jesus often withdrew to lonely places and prayed. (Luke 5:15–16)

Demands
Retreat
Engagement
Withdrawal
Healing
Renewal

I began to see the rhythm of His life—exhale, inhale, exhale, inhale. . . .

No wonder I was out of breath! I'd been trying to run a race without proper breathing. I needed time away to exhale anxiety, stress, and noise, and I needed solitude to inhale certainty, calm, and renewal.

———

That night we had a three-hour campfire time of praise and worship as we shared what each of us had experienced during our solos. It was exhilarating and encouraging, just what we needed. On Catalina we began to embrace solitude as we got away from the clamor and listened for His still, small voice. Eugene Peterson says, "Everybody else is noisier than God."[1]

Then, after returning to the mainland, we had dialogues with others who asked questions like, "Who was the speaker?"

"Nobody."

"Did you have a worship band?"

"No."

"Was the schedule exciting?"

"No."

"Accommodations good?"

"No."

"Sounds terrible."

"Best retreat I've been on—we met Jesus!"

Why do we choose to live hurriedly and worriedly . . . over-stimulated . . . up late, up early . . . never resting, ever rushing? If Christ is the Way, why aren't we following His example? Henri Nouwen wrote:

> If we don't pause to listen to God, we aren't taking the spiritual life seriously. But when we've eliminated outer distractions—people to talk with, books to read, TV to watch, or phone calls to make—we feel uneasy. That's because those *outer* distractions have shielded us from *interior* noises—doubts, anxieties, fears, bad memories, unresolved conflicts, angry feelings, and impulsive desires—that now surface in full force. We're bombarded by these thoughts and feelings that emerge from hidden areas of our mind. They can be so unsettling that we can hardly wait to get busy again![2]

I call this "being ambushed by myself." Instead of pulling away, being silent, and reconnecting with the Source, *in order to* bring my inner disturbances to Him, I allow the outer to drown out the interior, ruining the possibility of serenity and reflection. This is self-defeating behavior.

We soothe ourselves by wistfully saying, "If only I had more time."

But God has given us twenty-four hours *every day*—how couldn't that be enough?

Tim Stafford states it succinctly:

> We don't need more time; we need a way to stop and rest. Our world will bring us no relief. Genuine rest will have to come from inside us. It will have to become a core value, shaping our lives because of its spiritual power. We make rest a core value through family culture. If we manage that, we will do great service to other harried families, by witnessing to another way.[3]

ANOTHER WAY

Back to the Sermon on the Mount. After admonishing His listeners for chasing after the wrong things, Jesus tells them the right "thing" to pursue.

God.

And then He shows them how to do it. God never expects us to do anything for which He doesn't provide the resources.

Why did Jesus take time to show His followers how to pray? So that we might be connected to the heavenly Father. This is what it's all about; that's why Jesus came. *Connecting.* Because God wants to connect with us, He sent Jesus as a sacrifice and as an example of how to stay in abiding contact. In fact, the language of the text of Matthew 6:9 means, "This is how to remain in continual communication with God."

> Our Father in heaven,
> hallowed be your name,
> your kingdom come,
> your will be done
> on earth as it is in heaven. (v. 9–10)

The first step toward discovering another way is, "It's not

about me." This may be the hardest conversation you'll ever have with yourself, but you have to start there. *It's all about God.* It's about making Him the focus—acknowledging Him as King over every area of your life. Then, and only then, can you begin to understand that "your kingdom come" means *anything that promotes Him as Lord.* This is not some obscure future principality; in my life, the advancement of God's kingdom is about the decisions I make today, especially those that affect my family.

THREE KINDS OF FAMILIES

I've observed three kinds of homes. The first kind is *child-centered,* focused on making kids into kings and queens (or at least princes and princesses). The emphasis? Adding things to their lives that will allegedly make them more comfortable and enriched, whether expensive experiences, items, or programs, all designed to give them every "advantage" in life.

The second home is *parent-centered,* catering to the preferences and demands of one or two parents. Everything is designed primarily to accommodate the parent's busy schedule or demanding hobbies; weekends are patterned around indulgence or acquisition. This parent sees himself as king (or queen) of the castle and often uses terminology like "My house—my rules" and "My way or the highway." Some are super-religious, spending four or five nights each week at church or at church activities, dragging the kids along even when there isn't a class or program designed for them.

Neither of these homes helps us challenge the popular cultural current of being too busy. However, the third type does.

The *Christ-centered* home provides an antidote to worry. ("God will provide our daily bread.") It provides an alternative to hurry. ("Be still, and know that I am God.") It offers relief from stress. ("I will deliver you from the evil one.")

When we place children at the center, we breed insecurity in them—ultimately, they know intrinsically that they don't belong there.

When we place parents at the center, we breed resentment in the children—they definitely know that we don't belong there.

But when we place Christ in a position of honor at the center of our family, every family member can settle into his or her God-designed role. We don't have to fight over who's going to be king, for we're all under the authority of "Our Father in heaven—*your* kingdom come, *your* will be done."

Acknowledging and embracing the preeminence of God's kingdom in our family gives us a long-range point of view. We don't have to stress over daily concerns that He's promised to handle. Instead we can focus on glorifying Him with our lives, which helps us temper our desire for approval, achievement, and acquisition. With a kingdom mindset, our ambition is directed toward crowning Him, not exalting ourselves. With a kingdom mindset, our achievement is paced—we don't always have to produce, and in fact, we can rest while knowing that we're following His example. With a kingdom mindset within our families we can effectively deal with acquisition through an evaluative approach that asks, "Does *this* build the kingdom of God?"

CHRIST'S SERMON OUTLINE

The Sermon on the Mount teaches several principles that we can apply to building His kingdom in our families and finding relief from the hamster wheel of senseless activity. Here are four.

(1) Travel Light

Forgive us our debts, as we also have forgiven our debtors. (Matthew 6:12)

When we forgive others, we let go of our burdensome forty-two-inch suitcase of resentment and are liberated. Families should be laboratories for forgiveness. Our kids need to hear from us, "I'm sorry—will you forgive me?" They already *know* we aren't perfect; they're waiting to see if we're authentic. Requesting forgiveness and encouraging our kids to do the same deposits integrity into our family.

(2) Invest Right

> Do not store up for yourselves treasures on earth, where moth and rust destroy, and where thieves break in and steal. But store up for yourselves treasures in heaven, where moth and rust do not destroy, and where thieves do not break in and steal. For where your treasure is, there your heart will be also. (Matthew 6:19–21)

All our work, all our investments, all our striving . . . for what? So that it can be lost?

Moths don't discriminate. They'll eat a two-thousand-dollar suit or a two-dollar scarf. It's all food to them.

Rust never sleeps. If you have a beautiful yacht, right now rust is eating away at some part of your pride and joy.

Discouraging. And it gets worse:

All of what we own is susceptible to theft and decay.

So what are we supposed to do?

Hold things loosely. Be a good steward of what you have, but realize you're a manager of it, not the owner: It all belongs to God.

Also, *do not hoard—send it ahead.* Make sure you invest a percentage of your income in kingdom-building ventures in your church, in missions, and in nonprofits that reflect your values. Teach your children to follow your example.

One way we've tried to train our kids is through a "get one, give one" principle. If one of us gets a new outfit, we go through our closet and pick something we don't wear to give to The Salvation Army. This keeps us from accumulating too many clothes and serves as a gentle reminder that we can help others by not hoarding for ourselves.

(3) Chill!

Do not worry about your life, what you will eat or drink; or about your body, what you will wear. Is not life more important than food, and the body more important than clothes? Look at the birds of the air; they do not sow or reap or store away in barns, and yet your heavenly Father feeds them. Are you not much more valuable than they? *Who of you by worrying can add a single hour to his life?* (Matthew 6:25–27, emphasis added)

Jesus' list is comprehensive. "Do not worry about your life" is inclusive enough, but just to cover the bases, He breaks it down. "Don't worry about what you will eat or drink." We place *so* much emphasis on food trends, dining out, eating the right products, and so on.

Then He deals with another obsession—our bodies. Consider the current rage of makeover TV shows, plastic surgery, extreme diets, personal trainers, miracle dentistry, and plastic surgery; we can do such an overhaul on our body that we seemingly come out with a new one.

Christ also highlights a cultural fascination in addressing fashion: "What will I wear?" To capture the emotion, energy, and money that goes into clothes, shoes, purses, and accessories, look at a gossip magazine. Between the covers will be dozens of photos of the latest fads adorning high-profile celebrities.

Should we worry about our clothes? Jesus says no.

Should we have no regard for what we wear—should we go to church or to the office in our bathrobe? No. There's a difference between concern and worry; concern means to give thought to without being consumed by, while worry is being controlled by anxiety.

TONY'S FASHION TIPS

I was one of the speakers at a conference in Portland, and the organizers invited some of us to a Chinese restaurant for dinner. We met in front of the hotel and crammed into a taxi; I sat next to Tony Campolo—renowned author, sociology professor, and popular speaker.

"How come I always see you wearing your blue blazer, khaki pants, and blue oxford shirt? You do change, don't you?"

"As much as I sweat, you'd know if I didn't," he joked. "I take Jesus' words seriously, not to fret about what you'll wear. I used to worry, 'Will I make a fashion faux pas?' But now I wear the same thing. What you see is what you get."

"Like a uniform?"

"Exactly. Life is too short to be worried about fashion. I've got bigger fish to fry."

"So you bring matching outfits when you travel?"

"Yeah, I bring one blazer, two or three blue shirts, a couple of khaki pants, and I'm set. Takes all the stress from it."

Who of you by worrying can add a single hour to your life? The words of Christ replayed in my mind.

Jesus calls us to learn from the birds. I've never seen a bird anxiously poring over *The South Beach Diet* cookbook. I've never seen one checking out his backside in a mirror to see if he was too fat. I've never seen one clicking at a PDA.

We must entrust our worries to our Father. My encouragement to you? Become a bird brain! (Not a birdbrain.)

(4) Bloom Where You're Planted

> And why do you worry about clothes? See how the lilies of the field grow. They do not labor or spin. Yet I tell you that not even Solomon in all his splendor was dressed like one of these. . . .
>
> So do not worry, saying, "What shall we eat?" or "What shall we drink?" or "What shall we wear?" For the *pagans run after all these things,* and your heavenly Father knows that you need them. (Matthew 6:28–29, 31–32, emphasis added)

Lilies don't strain to accomplish their best. They don't labor to be more lily-like. They allow the natural, Creator-shaped rhythms to emerge without forcing or fretting, submitting to God's growth plan for them. They don't try to be an oak, a sagebrush, or even a rose. They recognize that God is the Master Gardener, so they bloom in glory and splendor.

Why do pagans run after "all these things" about which Jesus orders us not to worry?

A pagan is someone who holds and applies a naturalistic, materialistic philosophy. Many pagans are hedonistic, living out a beer-commercial-slogan type of world view based on *What brings me pleasure, right now?*

A pagan approach is destined to running. Pleasure is elusive—you have to stay on-the-go to find it, and just when you find it, it slips away. The world's pleasure *is* pleasurable, but only for a fleeting moment. Ultimately, it doesn't satisfy. If you want to be on the run, chase after what popular culture says are the goals; if you want to fulfill your purpose and bring splendor to your environment, learn to bloom where you're planted.

But seek first his kingdom and his righteousness, and all these things will be given to you as well. (Matthew 6:33)

A KINGDOM-BUILDING FAMILY

Seeking God's kingdom means putting Him first; a kingdom-building family gives God priority with its relationships and its values. We treat each other as "joint heirs." We submit our individual concerns and preferences to benefit the whole. We build our family values on our foundation of faith.[4]

A kingdom perspective delivers us from the tyranny of the urgent. It gives us a long-term viewpoint. It helps us not worry about or be reactive to momentary crises. Instead of stressing or fleeing, ask, "How does God, the Master Gardener, want me to not run after something else but put my roots down and grow from *this* current challenge?"

Remember: *It usually isn't about doing more. It's usually about doing less.* It's usually about embracing calmness as a friend (instead of regarding it as an adversary) and learning to cease from distracting activity. Kingdom-focused people—kingdom-focused families—are refreshing.

God said, "Be still, and know that I am God," not, "Scurry around and see if you can find me."

BEYOND THE CASTLE

He is happiest, be he king or peasant, who finds his peace at home. (Johann Wolfgang von Goethe)

All good kingdoms have clear boundaries, defined roles, common rituals, and widespread safety. Boundaries define where our kingdom ends and another begins. Families need clear boundaries to be healthy and successful.

Again, you might start by setting a boundary regarding a family Sabbath—a designated time to break from routine for rest and reconnection. Tim Stafford explains the importance:

> Rest is not a rule for us, then, something that we have to observe in a certain precise manner. Rather rest is a human need, like sleep and food—and even more, rest is an opportunity. The Scriptures say that God himself rested on the seventh day of creation (Genesis 2:2–3). That changes the whole concept of rest. God was certainly not tired or overstimulated. Why then did he rest? It must be for the same reason that he created the universe: because it was in his nature so to do. God rests, and we all can rest. Rest is built into the rhythm of existence, like the still between the waves. We honor God when we imitate his restfulness.[5]

Toward developing your family Sabbath, here are a few guidelines in a simple acrostic: REST.

R: *Relationships.*

Structure the time for people, not production. The main idea is having enough time to rest, to enjoy each other's company, and to strengthen relationships with family members. We show honor to God and to family when we set aside time to be with them.

E: *Escape from the routine.*

Make your family Sabbath unique, fun, and anticipated. If an entire day is too much, start with, say, a two-hour block. If you're stuck for ideas, set some parameters with your kids and then ask for their input. Try serving special foods, light candles, use the china and crystal, and play music in the background during the meal.

S: *Spiritual.*

Include spiritual elements. Show how God relates to our lives and is concerned with the details of our existence. It doesn't have to be a long, drawn-out Bible study; center on a key idea with a verse or two, or a story. (For suggestions, see the appendix.)

T: *Technology free.*

Turn off TVs, computers, phones, iPods, stereos, PDAs, and everything else, then substitute with activities that renew you. I know of one family that on Saturday night goes to church and out to dinner, then on Sunday morning goes surfing together. None of them ever misses it, including the three teenagers!

A family that learns to rest is refreshing.

What's fun for your family? What renews your family? Effective rest does *not* necessitate passivity. It's not about sitting in the living room staring at each other or at the walls.

The anticipation of a family Sabbath and other routines facilitates a predictable pace for our family, helping to define who we are and who we are not. We strengthen our identity, we emphasize the principles we value, and we reinforce a sense of belonging. Consistent family traditions build family community, presenting a place where each family member is known, loved, and needed.

As Otis Ledbetter and I wrote in *Family Traditions:*

> We live in a hurried and transient culture, but the practice of traditions gives our children stability, dependability, and shared memories. These three qualities help people feel connected in relationship and community. This is critical in a rootless society. Traditions, by their very nature, are boundaries: "This is the way we do it. We don't do it that way." Predictable traditions increase our children's sense of personal security because they define a place to stand without being too rigid.[6]

DISCUSSION QUESTIONS

Parent to Parent

1. Would you be interested in a silent retreat on an island? Why or why not?
2. What can we learn from Christ's model of getting away by himself?
3. What are some practical examples of Eugene Peterson's comment that "everybody else is noisier than God"?
4. Of the three kinds of families described above (child-, parent-, and Christ-centered), which depicts your family, and why?
5. What are pagans pursuing when they run? What are some ways we can be like lilies and bloom where we're planted?

Parent and Child

1. Pretend you have a thirty-hour day. On a piece of paper, draw a pie diagram and slice the pie according to how you would spend it. Both parent and child should make a "new-day pie," then discuss it. Focus on what you would do if you had six extra hours in a day.
2. Ask, "What activities are fun *and* restful for you? What activities can we do as a family that will help us relax and enjoy each other?"
3. Ask, "What are some ways we can avoid being wrapped up in food, fashion, and body shape?"

CHAPTER FIFTEEN

Family Heartprint

One of my favorite scenes from the life of Christ is when He cuddled the kids:

> People were bringing little children to Jesus to have him touch them, but the disciples rebuked them. When Jesus saw this, he was indignant. He said to them, "Let the little children come to me, and do not hinder them, for the kingdom of God belongs to such as these. I tell you the truth, anyone who will not receive the kingdom of God like a little child will never enter it." And he took the children in his arms, put his hands on them and blessed them. (Mark 10:13–16)

You may have seen movies where the blue-eyed Messiah in the flowing white robe leisurely sits on a rock while the children quietly and cautiously approach and sit at His feet. I had this same picture in my mind. I think it may also have to do with the art that was in my children's Bible or famous paintings I've seen in a museum.

It's the wrong image.

These were real kids, not passive paintbrush models. They were young and rambunctious, noisy and vigorous. In the agrarian society of the time they probably had dirt under their fingernails, grimy sandaled feet, and were sweaty and sticky from running around outdoors.

They pushed past the adults and lunged toward Jesus, wriggling and shoving to get the closest.

Jesus picked up these gritty, boisterous, unsophisticated children and placed them on his lap! He ran his fingers through matted hair, smiling and speaking softly.

"Preposterous!" exclaimed one disciple.

"Disgusting!" echoed another, stepping toward them.

"We have to make time for the VIPs," echoed a third, gesturing to the influential elite he'd invited for a private session with Jesus. "Shoo them away. They're children!"

"Exactly," Jesus replied. "For God's sake, and for the sake of these, I came." He hugged the four-year-old raven-haired boy on his lap—the one with the cowlick and dirt-smudged cheeks. Jesus smiled and repeated, "The kingdom of God is like this little child."

The boy leaned into Jesus' chest, then began picking his nose. Now that's reality!

I'd like to see a painting of *that* in the Art Institute of Chicago!

I'm not trying to be gross; I'm trying to bring life's plainness into view. You know that if it was your preschooler (or mine) sitting on Jesus' lap, this could happen. (It probably did.) The point is, Jesus said the kingdom of God belongs to such as these: *the kids!*

I find this encouraging. We don't have to be refined, acculturated adults to enjoy a kingdom perspective with our families.

I find it liberating. We don't have to follow the pace and demands of society. Children don't know all the rules of etiquette and decorum.

I find it realistic. Maybe it's my simple brain, but I can understand childlike behavior. My wife says I'm an expert on this topic!

Jesus was saying to receive the kids *as they are*. They don't have to clean up, fix up, grow up, or fake up to be accepted. The Creator of the universe accepts them *as is*.

When we receive our kids as is, we reflect Christ's uncondi-
tional love, shaped by His outrageous grace. Christ could see past
the façade into the heart. He wasn't concerned with income, social
status, or clothes. He wasn't even concerned with cleanliness. He
was concerned with their hearts.

I think there is a huge lesson here for parents. To follow
Christ's example, I don't need to be stressed about how my children look or how they perform on the outside, but I do need to
be concerned with their hearts. Aligning their hearts with God
means I can leave the externals up to Him.

When we do this, we're allowing for:

- Process—"You can be an unrefined child on the path to
  maturity. You don't have to be perfect."
- Childlike discovery—"We won't squelch your natural curiosity
  and openness to learn."
- Individual differences—"Not everybody has to look alike,
  behave exactly the same, or like the same things. You can be
  you!"

Children have a way of doing their own thing; this natural
comedy and spontaneity has spawned several hilarious family
shows on TV. Kids are impulsive, haven't learned all the rules, and
haven't been socialized into subdued adults.

I'm not saying you should let your kids be savages. I am saying that on the road to growing civil young adults who contribute
to community and to the kingdom of God, have some fun. *Don't
worry about making your child into a cookie-cutter ideal of the perfect Christian kid.* Allow for and affirm differences.

Tim Kimmel writes:

> Grace-based families are homes where children are given:
> (1) The freedom to be different
> (2) The freedom to be vulnerable

(3) The freedom to be candid

(4) The freedom to make mistakes.[1]

THE GOOD-ENOUGH PARENT

I used to struggle with feeling I wasn't *enough* as a father. I didn't do what I'd heard other *good Christian dads* did (although I'd never actually seen them do it).

We prayed with our daughters, read them Bible stories and other stories when they were little, took them to church on Sundays. Our church had a midweek Bible club program that "all the kids belong to," we were told. We felt pressure to enroll Nicole as a kindergartner, and even though we thought she was already busy enough with soccer and art lessons, we gave in.

After a month or two, her leader, Sally, called to say, "Nicole is not keeping up with the required memory work. She's still in the beginner's book. Do you know that we require the kids to memorize a verse every week?"

"Yes, but we want her to do it at her own pace," Suzanne explained. "She has enough pressure. We want her to enjoy the club and not feel she has to be competitive with spiritual issues. She can compete at soccer."

Sally was dumbfounded. "But she'll fall behind. . . . Umh . . . she's not following the program. The schedule requires it. Don't you want her to—"

"Thanks for your concern. Good-bye."

Sally liked the club program because everything was defined. A tight schedule every week. Forms to be followed. A routine to be maintained. Boxes to check. A perfectionist's dream.

After some time, Nicole complained about the program, so we pulled her out—it was too much for her.

I kept in contact with Sally and was always impressed with her organization and neatness. Her children were impeccably dressed and well mannered, excelling in Bible club and winning awards. Her house was immaculate, and they were seen as the "perfect Christian family." Christmas letters chronicled their accomplishments and goodness. After being in her home, admiring the flawless family photos with matching smiles and matching outfits, I felt inadequate and *not quite good enough.*

It seemed all perfect in Sally-world.

Until her first child became a teenager.

Hannah wouldn't fit into Sally's cookie-cutter mold. She wouldn't go to the "stupid Bible club" and eventually didn't want anything to do with a "church full of posers." Sally put the screws to her, clamping down, shrinking her world.

At sixteen, Hannah bolted and ran away.

The perfection of the Sally-world bubble burst.

What went wrong?

I think it began when Sally mistook parenting for manufacturing. She chose a template for her kids and demanded they conform to it. She didn't allow for differences—even God-given ones.

Grace-based parents do allow for their children's differences; in fact, they study their children to discover them. When I speak of differences, I'm not talking about varying moral standards. I'm not saying, "If your kid is into lying, let him do it." I'm saying to allow your kids to express themselves in a morally acceptable way even if it's not your preferred method. It may annoy or embarrass you, and that may be exactly why they like it!

Allowing our kids to express themselves with a pace of life that works for them is affirming and embracing their heartprint. If you insist that your child have and maintain the same heartprint as you or anyone else, you're working counter to God's design. *You'll always be more effective as a parent if you work in cooperation with God's design for your child rather than against it.* God created you with the exact heartprint He wanted you to have for His purposes, not yours. He also gave you children with their unique heartprints to fulfill His purposes for their lives.

DON'T BE TOO HARD ON YOURSELF

I like Tim Kimmel's way of saying that a grace-based family allows freedom to make mistakes. This is a profoundly biblical principle: The whole concept of grace implies that we need forgiveness for our missteps. What a great place to learn about the grace of God—right in front of us, at home. I like to define grace as *love in relationship,* not allowing anything to hinder the relationship but keeping it strong in love. In fact, we believe this so strongly that on the wall in the entryway of our home we have scripted: "Grace sees beauty in everything."

As we attempt to understand our own heartprint and that of our child, we might make mistakes. We might fail. We might misunderstand. But let's remember to stay free with grace, not condemning ourselves as we learn. Discovery is more art than science. As you search to comprehend and apply these concepts, you'll need some finesse. You can't simply follow a formula and get guaranteed results. You'll make some blunders, but you will also have success.

Grace underlies the process of trial and error. No failure is truly final; failure is only final when we seek to blame someone else, for when we blame, we stop learning. Grace allows us to keep learning. Grace helps us discover the beauty in everything.

FOCUSING ON HEARTPRINTS

By now, you may have decided on your heartprint. You may be a Cruiser who enjoys unrushed thoroughness; a Walker who prefers unhurried connection time and steady progression; a Runner motivated and fulfilled by appointments and activities; or a Biathlete who likes a variety of moving quickly and then resting to catch your breath.

Whatever your preferred heartprint, God has designed it for you. You don't have to aspire to a faster or slower life pulse. *None is more valuable or more spiritual than another.* They are simply different.

Remember, also, that while most people have a preferred pace—their primary heartprint—they also have a secondary heartprint, one that might be circumstantially or situationally needed. For example, you're a Runner. A death in your extended family means traveling back to the farm for the memorial service. Suddenly the calendar seems to have regressed thirty years . . . the days drag on . . . outside of the ceremony, *there's nothing to do.* You feel anxious but know it's not appropriate to be marching around in pursuit of cell service or setting up a workstation. How do you handle it? Perhaps by summoning your inner Walker or Cruiser and allowing yourself to go slower than you normally prefer.

Again, because your family is a combination of heartprints, you may not only have a representative from each of the four types, but if each individual has a primary and secondary type, you might also have eight heartprints in a family of four. If you desire, go back to further examine the Heartprint Quadrant (in chapter 11). Write your name or initials in the boxes that signify your primary and perhaps secondary heartprint, then write the initials of your spouse and children where you think most appropriate. (See also extra diagram copies in the appendix). If you still experience uncertainty or simply would like additional insight and understanding, read over the chapters on heartprints with your child, stopping to ask and answer questions, progressing only at a pace that benefits you both. Move slowly, think creatively, and interact lovingly.

The If/Then Heartprints Chart

If you feel you have little or no clue on how to relate to your child who is either very much like you or remarkably different than you, consider the following chart for ideas. I call this the *If/Then Heartprints Chart,* as in, for instance, "If I'm a Cruiser parent, then what should I do or avoid doing with my Runner child?"

	CRUISER PARENT	WALKER PARENT	RUNNER PARENT	BIATHLETE PARENT
CRUISER CHILD	+ Find fun projects to do together − Encourage functioning differently than you	+ Suggest doing things with you − Belittle fascination for detail	+ Involve him in planning family days − Rush him as he works	+ Connect with her on your rest cycles − Criticize her lack of adventure
WALKER CHILD	+ Plan outings together − Get upset if he forgets an item on your list	+ Establish routines, traditions − Get into a rut or avoid spontaneity	+ Affirm dependability, loyalty − Let her retreat away from new friendships	+ Affirm consistency, steadiness − Push her into scary experiences

RUNNER CHILD	+ Support her sport/ activity with organizational skills (yours) − Over-worry about her doing too much	+ Affirm his social skills and his aptitudes − Avoid bringing up difficult issues	+ Enjoy entertaining friends together − Plan the party; find a Cruiser to help you	+ Learn new outdoor skills and activities together − Overbook, or race without rest
BIATHLETE CHILD	+ Learn his start and stop rhythms − Squelch his creativity and impulsiveness	+ Share a "faster than you prefer" activity − Fear her curiosity or questioning	+ Allow rest stops and "pointless diversions" − Feed a "need for victory"	+ Explore new endeavors together − Confuse each other with variety

Key: **+** = What to try to do
     − = What to try to avoid

Why spend so much time and energy looking at your family's pace? Every family is different. You need to figure out who *your* family is; no other approach will work for you.

For example, many Christians think that spiritual training is (and needs to be) sitting down regularly to read and study the Bible together, but they struggle mightily because this template simply does not fit their family. Turn this around: Instead of trying to change your family to meet an ideal of how to spiritually train your children, change the application of your ideal to serve who your family is. It's not a matter of whether *training* is needed (it is); you need to choose the right *tools* for your family, and this necessarily takes into account their unique heartprints and heartprint combinations.[2]

If you're tempted to compare your family's pace with another family's, resist—this will only lead to frustration and/or discouragement. Focus your attention on *your* family, in all of its situations and routines. Some families, for instance, have a totally different shared heartprint on vacation than they do the rest of the year. The ones who are aware of this make accommodations when they plan their vacation.

I've written this book because I have a passion for families. I'm concerned that in our hectic pace we haven't been able to preserve time for relationships. I'm not saying we're all going too fast; even though most of us are moving quickly, some families are doing so while handling it well. How do they do it?

They make time for each other. In spite of fast pace and much activity, they still carve out sufficient time to stay connected. Again, the theme is, *whatever your pace, make sure you stay connected.* And if you can't connect, you probably need to slow down.

Daniel Siegel and Mary Hartzell offer sharp insight:

> The positive connects we have had with others in or outside of our families serve as a core resilience that may have helped us to weather the storm of difficult times in the past. Fortunately, even those of us who had quite difficult childhoods often have had some positive relationships during those years that can offer a seed of strength to help us overcome early adversity.
>
> We are not destined to repeat the patterns of our parents or our past. Making sense of our lives enables us to build on positive experiences as we move beyond the limitations of our past and create a new way of living for ourselves and for our children. Making sense of our own lives can help us to provide our children with relationships that promote their sense of well-being, give them tools for building an internal sense

of security and resilience, and offer them interpersonal skills that enable them to make meaningful, compassionate connections in the future.[3]

Sometimes our lives seem crazy because we've yet to make sense of them. By slowing down, by taking time to look at the issue of pace and its impact on our family, we have the opportunity to discover our own heartprint. We're able to come to terms with the optimum speed for operating our lives. When we're at peace with ourselves, our pace, and our history, we create an environment of connection for our children. Providing them with a clear sense of self and a place of security affords a pathway for their healthy growth.

Being an effective parent in the new millennium might have less to do with activities, enrichment, and a full schedule, and more to do with following the pattern of the One who said no to the demands and props of the adult world, who sat down and said, "Let the children come to me, and do not hinder them."

It might mean stopping our activity and cuddling with our kids. Find out for yourself whether it really could be that simple.

DISCUSSION QUESTIONS

Parent to Parent

1. What do you imagine really happened when Jesus took time out to be with the children (Mark 10:13–16)? What does this model for parents today?
2. Discuss how applying Tim Kimmel's four elements of grace-based families can help. Children are given:
    1. The freedom to be different
    2. The freedom to be vulnerable

3. The freedom to be candid
4. The freedom to make mistakes

3. Discuss where you see yourself and your children on the Heartprint Quadrant (chapter 11 and appendix).

4. What are some other ideas for relating to a child with a heartprint different than yours? Discuss the *If/Then Heartprints Chart* (pp. 198–199) and formulate suggestions.

5. What changes are you going to make in your family life as a result of going through this book? What changes in your personal life?

Parent and Child

1. Ask, "What makes you happy?" and "What's ideal for you?"

2. Examine the Heartprint Quadrant and ask, "Where do you see me on this?" "Where do you see your brother and/or sister?" "Where do you see yourself, most of the time?"

3. Ask, "Would you say that as a family we go too slow, too fast, it's always changing, or it's at just the right speed? Why?"

APPENDIX

The following are twenty ideas—"Hang Time" Suggestions— for *no-agenda time* with your child at each stage of development. Casual, relaxation-based hangout time as a family is an essential antidote to our culture's hectic pace. This is a countercultural discipline. It's not about learning, competing, achieving, or being recognized; it's about resting and connecting. You don't pay for it, but it's an investment that pays off.

Preschool

1. Take a "Three-Foot Walk" and observe what life looks like from that perspective. Show your child how high thirty-six inches is, then say, "We're going on an adventure for anything interesting that's this high or lower." Focus on and talk about only those things. (By the way, medical research reports that while walking, the body actually secretes brain chemicals that counteract stress.)
2. Develop an end-of-evening routine that involves pleasant rituals your child will anticipate. Play a favorite song to announce bedtime. Read stories, talk about the day's events, and pray together. Being consistent will help your child look forward to this time alone with you as you focus on him.
3. On weekends, try fixing special breakfasts that take more time, like pancakes or French toast. As you lick syrup from your fingers, talk about things that are "sweet" (good); things that are "sticky" (good or bad, i.e., sticky situations); things that are "sour" (bad or unpleasant).

Make it more a conversational game than a lesson.
4. Buy some clay or Play-Doh and create together.

Elementary School

5. Schedule time to hang as a family. For instance, you might reserve Sunday afternoon for family lunch, family nap, family walk, and family games. Protect this time; everything else works around it.
6. Develop an anti-boredom Rx. With your children, make a list of at least ten things they can do when they feel bored. When appropriate, join them with the prescription.
7. Movie Trivia. Rent or play one of your favorite family videos, but this time have each person write three trivia questions on a three-by-five card. Enjoy popcorn during the movie, then shuffle the cards and take turns seeing who can answer the most questions. Appoint one person to be the moderator. Award the champ (individual or team, if you have a large family) with licorice or other candy.
8. Go to a thrift store and give each family member a few dollars with the instruction to "buy a costume we'll use in a play." Return home and try them on. Develop character biographies for each family member's character. Write down at least seven facts about each ("He's a superhero disguised as a butcher," etc.). Write a play that uses all the characters and their traits. Then act it out! You may (or may not) want to videotape it. Ad-libbing is encouraged!
9. Go on a family camping trip—to your backyard. Sleep under the stars. If you can, roast marshmallows and make s'mores. Enjoy late-night chats and munchies (without brushing your teeth!).

Middle School

10. Invite a few friends to join your family in a game of Sardines. Appoint one person to be "it." Turn out all the lights in the house; "it" hides somewhere. Everyone else, one or more at a time, gradually finds her and hides with her, smashed together like sardines. Last person to find the group gets to pick the next "it."

11. Make an indoor (and/or outdoor!) mini-golf course with cardboard, scrap wood, soda cans, pieces of carpet, et cetera. Use real putters or make them from pieces of 1x1 boards, available at any home improvement center. (Sometimes mini-golf courses sell old putters.)

12. Go to a music store together and listen to one track of each person's favorite music (using headphones). Yes, this means the kids have to listen to one of their parents' songs!

13. Family Retro Party. Pick a decade (sixties, seventies, or eighties) and have every family member dress accordingly (you may need to visit the thrift store). Pick an outlandish family-friendly video to watch together. Start with music from that era, some food popular during the decade, and, perhaps, a game (like Twister from the sixties). Then watch the video and make fun of the fashions (on screen *and* in the room!). Be sure to take photos.

14. Watch a popular teen show. Before it starts, determine three qualities that lead to healthy biblical living (e.g., telling the truth) and three mistakes that lead to unhealthy, unbiblical living (e.g., lying). Write them down. Before the show starts, have each family member predict the score: "Six qualities and seventeen mistakes," for example. Keep score with what's acted out or referred to on the show. The person with the closest guess wins a prize.

15. "Porta-Party." Get a cardboard box, then fill it with

candy, soda, decorations, noisemakers, and any party stuff from around the house or from the dollar store. Throw in a table game, pick an unsuspecting family of friends (with at least one middle school student), and surprise them with a visit. "We brought our Porta-Party to you; wanna join us?"

High School

16. Watch MTV with your teen for fifteen minutes without making any negative comments.

17. "Open Season." For one hour, when your teen is home, put down the paper, push back from your PC . . . basically look as open and available as possible. Sit on the couch, leaving a place next to you. If she asks, "What are you doing?" say, "Just relaxing. Join me if you like," and pat the couch. See what happens.

18. Drive somewhere in town, or to another city, that's markedly different from where you live. Have lunch and observe what's not the same as where you usually go. On the way home, talk about what you experienced.

19. Watch *The Passion of the Christ* and discuss, "What were the most meaningful scenes?" "What was most disturbing?" (etc.)

20. Browse popular teen magazines at the bookstore, then grab some ice cream and talk about one of the issues that seemed to be prevalent. For example, "What/who was popular last year but not this year? Why? What makes different things popular at different times?"

Heartprint Quadrant

High Activity

WALKER	RUNNER
Steady	*Fast*
Likes routine	Likes people
Loyal	Involved
Patient	Intuitive
Thoughtful	Influential
Avoids conflict	Takes risks
Consistent	Creative
CRUISER	BIATHLETE
Slow	*Fast and stop, fast and stop*
Likes details	Likes variety
Organized	Strategic
Industrious	Bold
Analytical	Leads
Makes lists	Curious
Compliant	Competitive

Low Activity   *Slow <*   Speed of Activity   *> Fast*

Heartprint Echocardiograms

Cruiser: Low level of activity; slow pace (low frequency)

Walker: Mid to high level of activity; slow to medium pace (low to medium frequency)

Runner: High level of activity; fast pace (high frequency)

Biathlete: Lower level of activity than Runner; pace alternates between very fast and very slow (various frequencies)

The If/Then Heartprints Chart

If you feel you have little or no clue on how to relate to your child who is either very much like you or remarkably different than you, consider the *If/Then Heartprints Chart.*

	CRUISER PARENT	WALKER PARENT	RUNNER PARENT	BIATHLETE PARENT
CRUISER CHILD	+ Find fun projects to do together − Encourage functioning differently than you	+ Suggest doing things with you − Belittle fascination for detail	+ Involve him in planning family days − Rush him as he works	+ Connect with her on your rest cycles − Criticize her lack of adventure
WALKER CHILD	+ Plan outings together − Get upset if he forgets an item on your list	+ Establish routines, traditions − Get into a rut or avoid spontaneity	+ Affirm dependability, loyalty − Let her retreat away from new friendships	+ Affirm consistency, steadiness − Push her into scary experiences
RUNNER CHILD	+ Support her sport/ activity with organizational skills (yours) − Over-worry about her doing too much	+ Affirm his social skills and his aptitudes − Avoid bringing up difficult issues	+ Enjoy entertaining friends together − Plan the party; find a Cruiser to help you	+ Learn new outdoor skills and activities together − Overbook, or race without rest

BIATHLETE CHILD	+ Learn his start and stop rhythms — Squelch his creativity and impulsiveness	+ Share a "faster than you prefer" activity — Fear her curiosity or questioning	+ Allow rest stops and "pointless diversions" — Feed a "need for victory"	+ Explore new endeavors together — Confuse each other with variety

Key: + = What to try to do
— = What to try to avoid

Hosting a Book Group

At my seminars I caution, "Don't attempt to parent alone—get help! Our kids use peer pressure on us: 'All the other parents are cool; they let their kids do it. Why not you?' Let's return the favor—let's start a parents' book group and support each other by reading and discussing materials that can help to improve our parenting."

Each chapter of *Connecting With Your Kids* ends with a "Parent to Parent" section because I designed it for use in book groups. I've discovered that parents who belong to a parenting-issues small group tend to be more equipped and not as stressed as others.

Here are a few tips to get you started.

1. Read the book and pass it along to a friend. Shared reading means you'll have a connection even as you begin the group.
2. Make a list of people you know who might be interested. It's ideal if the parents have children at the same stage: preschool, elementary, or teens. Look for participants at church, in your neighborhood, at school, or on your child's team. Include people from these various contacts for a lively group. Consider distributing a simple flyer

with a copy of the book cover and details about your group.

3. Some groups meet weekly, some every other week, some monthly. Choose the frequency that works best for you, and plan on at least an hour, but preferably ninety minutes. Plan for a minimum of six sessions and a maximum of fifteen (one session per chapter). Shorter is better for first-time book-group members.

4. Serve refreshments or meet at a café or bookstore that serves coffee. Start with a warm-up question that focuses on parenting and engages all members, like, "Describe a time when you felt so frantic as a parent that you wanted to freak out." After a few responses, thank everyone for coming and launch into the discussion questions. Don't stay on a question if general interest seems to be dragging.

5. Make sure you rotate the discussion by calling on different parents. If a parent isn't becoming involved, say, "Mary, I'd like to hear your thoughts on question four." Spend five to ten minutes with the warm-up question and five to eight minutes per discussion question (on average). This keeps dialogue going while also allowing time for the *hot issue* of the week—something you didn't plan for but usually begins with, "I can't believe what my kid did this week. . . ."

6. Keep the group from griping and complaining about their children—just a little of this prevention can lead to empathy and understanding. In other words, *none of you is alone in the challenge of parenting,* and too much whining makes a negative group. Get everybody on board with the warm-up question. Encourage everybody to be engaged in the discussion. Initiate with personal sharing and keep communication going by involving everyone who's willing to speak.

7. Conclude your time with, "What practical things can we try this week based on our discussion?" Have someone record these, and at the next session, ask, "Hey, how'd it go with your strategy for a twice-a-week family dinner?"
8. You can also include prayer and Bible reading (e.g., the selections mentioned in this book) if you want your group to be faith-oriented. Make sure prayer is optional—not everyone is willing to pray out loud. More parents are interested in a book group on parenting than a Bible study on parenting, especially those who don't attend church regularly.
9. Consider using the six-session companion DVD for *Connecting With Your Kids,* featuring twenty-minute presentations by the author and questions for even more in-depth discussion. (Available at *www.parentscoach.org.*)
10. Have fun! Encourage laughter and take time to get to know others in the group. Parenting is demanding. Sometimes the best way to get perspective and find renewal is by enjoying your connection with other parents.

RESOURCES

Books

Barna, George. *Real Teens: A Contemporary Snapshot of Youth Culture* (Ventura, Calif.: Regal, 2002).

―――. *Transforming Children Into Spiritual Champions: Why Children Should Be Your Church's #1 Priority* (Ventura, Calif.: Regal, 2003).

Burns, Jim. *Devotions on the Run: Pulling Out of the Fast Lane to Make Time With God* (Ventura, Calif.: Regal, 2004).

―――. *How to Be a Happy, Healthy Family* (Nashville: Thomas Nelson, 2001).

Cloud, Henry, and John Townsend. *Boundaries With Kids* (Grand Rapids: Zondervan, 2001).

Doherty, William J., and Barbara Z. Carlson. *Putting Family First: Successful Strategies for Reclaiming Family Life in a Hurry-up World* (New York: Henry Holt and Co., 2002).

Kimmel, Tim. *Grace-Based Parenting: Set Your Family Free* (Nashville: W Publishing Group, 2004).

———. *Little House on the Freeway* (Portland: Multnomah, 1987).

———. *Why Christian Kids Rebel: Trading Heartache for Hope* (Nashville: W Publishing Group, 2004).

Ledbetter, J. Otis, and Tim Smith. *Family Traditions: Practical, Intentional Ways to Strengthen Your Family Identity* (Colorado Springs: Cook Communications/Focus on the Family, 1998).

McGraw, Phil. *Family First: Your Step-by-Step Plan for Creating a Phenomenal Family* (New York: Free Press, 2004).

Rice, Wayne, ed. *Help! There's a Teenager in My House—A Troubleshooting Guide for Parents* (Downers Grove, Ill.: InterVarsity Press, 2005).

Rosenfeld, Alvin, and Nicole Wise. *The Over-Scheduled Child: Avoiding the Hyper-Parenting Trap* (New York: St. Martins Griffin, 2000).

Smith, Timothy. *The Seven Cries of Today's Teens: Hear Their Hearts, Make the Connection* (Nashville: Integrity, 2003).

Stafford, Tim. *Never Mind the Joneses: Building Core Christian Values in a Way That Fits Your Family* (Downers Grove, Ill.: InterVarsity Press, 2004).

Trent, John. *Be There! Making Deep, Lasting Connections in a Disconnected World* (Colorado Springs: WaterBrook, 2000).

———. *The Gift of the Blessing* (Nashville: Thomas Nelson, 1993).

———. *HeartShift: The Two-Degree Difference That Will Change*

Your Heart, Your Home, and Your Health (Nashville: Thomas Nelson, 2004).

Magazines

Christian Parenting Today is an excellent resource for practical, biblical advice for parents of infants to teens, written by nationally known experts. *www.christianparenting.net*

Parents of Teenagers, published by Lifeway, focuses on raising middle school and high school students; written in an easy-to-read style. *www.lifeway.com/magazines*

ParentLife, also published by Lifeway, deals with parenting younger children, birth to age twelve. Has practical, age-oriented categories, "Growth Spurts," and features like "Teaching Preschoolers to Pray."

Campus Life, a magazine for Christian teens and pre-teens, offers articles on teens making a difference and addresses practical issues such as "I'm Angry With God." *www.christianity today.com*

Web Sites

www.parentscoach.org Tim Smith's site for free parenting tips from the Parents' Coach; information on seminars and a store featuring Tim's CDs, DVDs, and books.

www.homeword.com Jim Burns's site with hundreds of free tips for parents and youth-workers. Updates on Jim's radio show and excellent resources at the store.

www.uyt.com Wayne Rice and his seminar team's site for the popular "Understanding Your Teenager" seminar. Features: e-letter, store, and information on upcoming seminars.

www.strongfamilies.com Dr. John Trent's site dedicated to building strong marriages and families through resources, seminars, and diagnostic tools.

www.familymatters.net Dr. Tim Kimmel's site with a fun "Dinner Dialogue" feature to enhance family meals; also contains information on his books, seminars, and audio/video products.

Videos

Drug-Proof Your Kids (by Jim Burns; Gospel Light). Learn how to reduce the risk of substance abuse with your teens.

Parenting Teens Positively (Jim Burns; Gospel Light). An upbeat and practical presentation by the nationally known expert and radio host.

Bringing Up Boys (James Dobson; Focus on the Family/Tyndale). Includes such topics as "Boys Will Be Boys," "The Trouble With Boys," "Wounded Spirits," "Routine Panic," "Questions From Parents and Grandparents," "Men R Fools," and "Boys R Fools, Too."

Connecting With Your Kids: How "Fast Families" Can Move From Chaos to Closeness (Tim Smith; Saddleback Church/Life Skills for American Families). Six sessions for parents' small groups. Comes with workbook.

The Passed-Thru-Fire Experience (Rick Bundschuh; Standard). A rite-of-passage curriculum guiding young men into manhood. Six sessions (book also available).

Understanding Your Teenager (Wayne Rice; UYT). A live DVD recording of the popular seminar for parents.

Seminars

Understanding Your Teenager (*www.uyt.com*) Wayne Rice and a team of youth-ministry and parenting experts in a 150-minute presentation for parents of preteens and teens. Humorous, practical, and hopeful.

John Trent presents two excellent seminars, *Strong Families in*

Stressful Times and *Strong Marriages in Stressful Times,* as well as other timely topics. (*www.strongfamilies.com*)

Tim Kimmel offers a variety of presentations like *Parenting 101.* Grace-based, character-driven models for raising confident, well-rounded kids, and other family issues. (*www.family matters.net*)

Tim Smith's seminars for parents include *Fast Families—How to Move From Chaos to Closeness* (based on this book); *The Relaxed Parent—Helping Your Kids Do More As You Do Less; Seven Cries of Today's Teens: Hear Their Hearts, Make the Connection;* and *Families That Rock! Building a Solid Foundation.* (*www.parentscoach.org*)

ENDNOTES

Chapter One

1. See Jeffrey M. Jones, "Parents of Young Children Are Most Stressed Americans" by Gallup News Service—Poll Analyses (11/8/02).
2. Ibid.
3. Alvin Rosenfeld, M.D., and Nicole Wise, *The Over-Scheduled Child: Avoiding the Hyper-Parenting Trap* (New York: St. Martins Griffin, 2000), 169.

Chapter Two

1. Dr. Phil McGraw, *Family First: Your Step-by-Step Plan for Creating a Phenomenal Family* (New York: Free Press, 2004), xiii–xiv.
2. William J. Doherty, Ph.D., and Barbara Z. Carlson, *Putting Family First: Successful Strategies for Reclaiming Family Life in a Hurry-up World* (New York: Henry Holt and Co., 2002), 15.
3. Tim Kimmel, *Little House on the Freeway* (Portland: Multnomah, 1987), 32–33.
4. Robert Coles, quoted by Barbara Vobejda and Paul Taylor in "Suddenly, A Pessimistic America," *The Washington Post* (11/6/90), A1.
5. "Family Dinners Improve Kids' Health and Grades" in the Ventura County *STAR* (11/13/04), E4.

Chapter Three

1. Jones, "Parents of Young Children."
2. Harville Hendrix, Ph.D., *Getting The Love You Want: A Guide for Couples* (New York: HarperPerennial, 1998) 15, 25.

Chapter Four

1. Jones, "Parents of Young Children."
2. Cited by Ken McAlpine, "The Young and the Restless" in *American Way* (12/03), 42.
3. Ibid., adapted.
4. Wayne Grudem, *Systematic Theology* (Grand Rapids: Zondervan/InterVarsity Press, 1994), 479.
5. Karen S. Patterson, "Extracurricular Burnout" in *USA Today* (11/19/02); as reported in NFI DAD e-mail, National Fatherhood Initiative (12/4/02).
6. McAlpine, *American Way*, 55, emphasis added.
7. "Poll Shows Kids Put Family Ahead of Buying Stuff" in *Pittsburg Post-Gazette*, as reported in the Ventura County *STAR* (3/4/04), A1.

Chapter Five

1. Ken McAlpine, "The Young and the Restless" in *American Way* (12/03), 55.
2. Dr. Eirini Flouri and Ann Buchanan, "Involved Fathers Key for Children" by the Economic & Social Research Council, March 2002. See *www.esrc.ac.uk*.
3. Harris Interactive Youthpulse: 3,878 online interviews conducted January 2001.
4. William Raspberry, "Environmentally Challenged" in the *Washington Post* (9/22/03); column discusses the report *Hardwired to Connect: The New Scientific Case for Authoritative Communities* by the Commission on Children at Risk (YMCA of the USA, Dartmouth Medical School, and Institute for American Values: 2003), 88.

Chapter Eight

1. For more ideas on planning meaningful traditions, see my book with J. Otis Ledbetter, *Family Traditions: Practical, Inten-*

tional Ways to Strengthen Your Family Identity (Colorado Springs: Focus on the Family, 1998).
2. Ibid., 32.

Chapter Nine

1. "Family Time, Family Values" by Mark Mellman, Edward Lazarus, and Allan Rivlin in *Rebuilding the Nest: A New Commitment to the American Family,* eds. David Blankenhorn, Steven Bayme, and Jean Bethke Elshtain (New York: Family Service American, 1990), 91.

Chapter Ten

1. Sally Weal, "Do you often feel ill on holiday . . . but never when you're at work? If so, you could be a victim of 'leisure sickness' " in *The Guardian* (11/26/02); see *www.travel.guardian.co.uk/news/story/0,7445,847874,00.html.*
2. See Randy Frazee, *Making Room for Life: Trading Chaotic Lifestyles for Connected Relationships* (Grand Rapids: Zondervan, 2003), 17.
3. Robert Putnam, *Bowling Alone: The Collapse and Revival of American Community* (New York: Simon & Schuster, 2000), 213.
4. Ibid., 115.
5. Dr. Phil McGraw, *Family First* (New York: Free Press, 2004), 42 (emphasis added).

Chapter Eleven

1. Adapted from Andrée A. Brooks, *Children of Fast-Track Parents* (New York: Viking, 1989), 29. Used by permission.
2. Tim Stafford, *Never Mind the Joneses—Building Core Christian Values in a Way That Fits Your Family* (Downers Grove, Ill.: InterVarsity Press, 2004), 87.
3. Rick Hampson, "Are They Relaxed Yet? Jersey town to find

out tonight—harried citizens take a night off" in *USA Today* (3/26/02), 1A.
4. Stafford, *Never Mind the Joneses,* 87.
5. For more information on planning rites of passage, check out *www.heritagebuilders.com* or Tim Smith and J. Otis Ledbetter, *Family Traditions: Practical, Intentional Ways to Strengthen Your Family Identity* (Colorado Springs: Focus on the Family/Cook Communications, 1998).

Chapter Twelve
1. Luke 10:38–42; John 11:17–45.
2. John 11:21–27.
3. Luke 10:39.
4. John 11:32.
5. John 12:3.
6. John 12:3.

Chapter Thirteen
1. *Napoleon Dynamite* DVD, Chapter 20. Fox Searchlight Pictures and Paramount Pictures, 2004.
2. See John Allen, "Ubuntu: An African Challenge to Individuality and Consumerism" in *Trinity News* (4/24/02); posted at *www.trinitywallstreet.org/news/article_62.shtml*
3. Randy Frazee, *Making Room for Life: Trading Chaotic Lifestyles for Connected Relationships* (Grand Rapids: Zondervan, 2003), 30–31.
4. See Ecclesiastes 3.
5. Benjamin Wiker, Ph.D. *To the Source* (12/8/04); see *www.tothesource.org.*

Chapter Fourteen
1. Eugene Peterson, "Dueling With Diversions" in *Men of Integrity: Your Daily Guide to the Bible and Prayer* (Carol Stream,

Ill.: Christianity Today/Promise Keepers), 12/2/04.
2. Ibid.
3. Stafford, *Never Mind the Joneses,* 161.
4. Galatians 3:26–29; Ephesians 4:15–16; 6:1–4.
5. Op. cit., 162–63.
6. Tim Smith and J. Otis Ledbetter, *Family Traditions,* 32.

Chapter Fifteen

1. Tim Kimmel, *Grace-Based Parenting: Set Your Family Free* (Nashville: W Publishing Group, 2004) 134.
2. See John Trent, Rick Osborne, and Kurt Bruner, *Parents' Guide to the Spiritual Growth of Children* (Wheaton, Ill.: Focus on the Family/Tyndale, 2000), 74.
3. Daniel J. Siegel, M.D., and Mary Hartzell, M.Ed., *Parenting from the Inside Out: How a Deeper Self-Understanding Can Help You Raise Children Who Thrive* (New York: Jeremy P. Tarcher/Penguin, 2004), 122–23.

ACKNOWLEDGMENTS

I am grateful for all who have supported me in my effort to strengthen families, notably:

- Denny and Allyson Weinberg for the vision to co-found our organization.
- Steve and Jana McBeth, Don and Sherry Armstrong, Steve and Robin Todd, Jack and Arlonne Monroe, Rich and Sheryl Bullock, and Steve and Debbie Carmandalian for their faithful service and wise counsel as directors.
- Greg Johnson, my co-conspirator, friend, cheerleader, and agent.
- Christopher Soderstrom, my editor, who knows his job and sports, and is fun to work with.
- Our daughters, Nicole and Brooke, for their enthusiasm and props (and letting me write about them!).
- My wife, Suzanne, who actually has the best ideas on parenting even though it's my name on the cover.